Withdrawn

Withdrawn

D0531590

# JANE'S
# NATO Warships Handbook

## Edited by Captain John Moore RN
# JANE'S

Computer typesetting by Method Limited, Epping, Essex

Printed in the United Kingdom by Butler and Tanner Ltd, Frome and London

**Cover illustration**: The frigate *Rheinland-Pfalz* ('Bremen' class) of the Federal
German Navy (*Foto-Flite*)

# CONTENTS

Indexes

# INTRODUCTION

Any study of the navies of NATO will result in an immediate sense of diversity. The only country in the Alliance without a maritime force of any kind is land-locked Luxembourg – the forces of the remainder vary from the considerable fleet of the USN to the tiny group of Icelandic coast-guard vessels. Some question the inclusion of the French Navy as part of the NATO system but, despite the staunchly nationalistic approach of that country, the present involvement of her naval and military staffs with those of the Alliance suggests that it would be prudent to add her forces to those of her neighbours. In the event of a war in Europe the USSR would have no more respect for neutrality than did Hitler's Germany.

The Warsaw Pact navies have one major advantage over those of NATO but suffer an equal disadvantage. All the Warsaw Pact countries are contiguous while the major NATO partner is separated from her European allies by 3000 miles of Atlantic Ocean. But the USA has immediate access to the high seas as do her major naval partners. The Warsaw Pact navies, on the other hand, suffer from major geographical constraints in the shape of the Greenland-UK island chain, the Danish Straits, the Turkish Straits and the islands of Japan. These problems have affected the types of ships and weapons developed by the Warsaw Pact where the requirements of strategy have been backed by generous financial resources and whose weapon development has been dictated by these needs. The NATO navies have, however, developed on the basis of national needs and these require some examination, based on a few basic assumptions.

The first of these is that no NATO nation is in any way self-sufficient as regards the need for raw materials and overseas trade. Some of this requirement can be met by the use of road and rail haulage and some by air transport – a total of about five percent. The remainder has to come by sea.

The second assumption stems from the capitalist system of competition and the comparatively high standard of living of those involved in the warship industry. The plain facts are that companies from all the countries of NATO are continually vying for foreign orders and the reaction of individual governments is to support this approach by supporting their own national sources. This provides local employment and, indirectly, gains votes.

The third assumption is that no NATO nation has, so far, achieved a concerted maritime policy which encompasses their naval, mercantile and fishing fleets as well as the numerous ancillary services concerned with transport, safety, navigation and the like. In the United Kingdom fourteen ministries are involved in one way or another. The urgent need, as NATO enters the span of the middle-aged, is for the individual governments to establish some form of overall national policy which can feed into a NATO central organisation. Such co-ordination is essential – at present the Alliance countries are wasting vast sums on research and development, a great deal of it on independent and parallel lines. Lack of flexibility and imagination in certain ministries is compounding this waste and perhaps Karl Marx was right when he prophesied that capitalism would encompass its own downfall.

So what is the current situation?

The navy of the USA, if it achieves the '600 ship' fleet to which it aspires, will have less than two thirds of the numbers in its inventory than it had at the end of the Vietnam conflict. Of these the nuclear propelled ships and submarines will be of the highest effectiveness, the amphibious forces will be reinforced but gaps will remain, particularly in the mine-countermeasures (MCM) ships.

The lack of any decisive naval policy in the United Kingdom allied with political procrastination have resulted in a steady decline in Britain's naval capability. Many designs are incompatible with a decreasing budget at a time when increased numbers are essential. Once again this is true of the MCM forces as well as the ASW ships and submarines.

In France, variations in the political climate have had less effect on programmes than financial restrictions. France has reorganised her world-wide commitments and is building ships adequate in capability, if not in numbers, to achieve self-sufficiency. While other countries haggle over the cost of a frigate or two France is building a nuclear propelled aircraft carrier with a second planned.

Well-planned programmes in both West Germany and Netherlands, centred on submarines, frigates, MCM vessels and naval aircraft are progressing steadily. In West Germany's case new submarine technology may soon result in major advances.

Both Norway and Denmark have small populations and low budgets. The former is placing emphasis on the modernisation of surface ships and the provision of new and larger submarines. Denmark has embarked on an imaginative programme from which the needs of many aspects of the fleet will be met from a standard hull design.

After years of wasteful indecision in Canada the first of a new class of destroyer is under construction while the remaining ships of the fleet are undergoing expensive modernisation. This is true of the three submarines which will require replacement before long.

The Belgian navy, though equipped with four frigates, is primarily concerned with mine-countermeasures.

The South-Western corner of European NATO consists of Portugal and Spain. The former has pressing financial problems and has spent a lengthy period deciding on the new MEKO 200 frigates as replacements for the more elderly of her 17 frigates. The much larger fleet of her Spanish neighbour is fortunate in having a well-found national ship-building industry to support it. A carefully graduated building programme is aimed at two carrier groups with strong submarine and amphibious forces. Spanish plans have to provide for operations in both the Atlantic and Mediterranean with national interests in North Africa and the Canary Islands.

Italy's interests are less widespread but still cover a long coastline on both sides of the country as well as Sardinia, Sicily and the islands in the Sicilian Channel. For this purpose a well-balanced fleet is being reinforced by new construction, the main point being that larger ships with greater range and capability are continuing to join the fleet and the size of submarines is steadily increasing. This tendency is to the advantage of NATO, providing greater flexibility of deployment in a crisis.

The Eastern Mediterranean is a vital area for the security of the Alliance. Turkey's eastern border marches with that of the USSR while, to the West, Turkish Thrace and Greece border Bulgaria, one of the more dependable Soviet satellites. The continual animosity which has existed for many years between these two NATO allies now centres on a number of quite trivial differences which appear of more importance to the authorities in Athens than to those in Ankara. However, as the interests of the two countries and those of the Alliance are centred in the same geographical area the two navies are of very similar composition, be they for national or NATO purposes. Submarines with a backing of destroyers, frigates, fast attack craft and amphibious forces figure largely in both inventories.

The forces of NATO are widely scattered, of diverse designs requiring very varied logistic support and with questionable compatibility in a number of areas. That they can work together is shown in numerous large and small exercises which are essential to the cohesion of the whole. No country has enough mine-countermeasures vessels, few have sufficient aircraft, either fixed or rotary wing, for surveillance and anti-submarine work while the overall total of available ships is never enough to meet the true force requirements of NATO's commanders.

Capt J. E. Moore, RN,
September 1986

# NATO FUNCTIONS AND STRUCTURE

The North Atlantic Treaty, signed in Washington on 4 April 1949, created an Alliance for collective defence as defined in Article 51 of the UN Charter.

MEMBER COUNTRIES: Belgium, Canada, Denmark, France, Federal Republic of Germany, Greece, Iceland, Italy, Luxembourg, Netherlands, Norway, Portugal, Spain, Turkey, United Kingdom and the United States. Combatant ships of all these countries are represented in this book except for Iceland, whose vessels are not considered to be within the scope of this volume, and Luxembourg. In 1966, France withdrew from the military organisation of NATO but has continued to make her forces available when required.

THE BASIC STRUCTURE OF NATO. As well as being a military alliance, NATO also provides for continuous co-operation and consultation in political, economic and other non-military fields. NATO forces are made up of three interlocking elements known as the NATO Triad. They are: Conventional forces, theatre nuclear forces to enhance the deterrent and defensive effect of the conventional forces, and United States and United Kingdom strategic nuclear forces which provide the ultimate deterrent. The highest decision-making body and forum for consultations within the Alliance is the North Atlantic Council (NAC), composed of representatives of the 16 member countries. The Defence Planning Committee (DPC) is composed of representatives of the member countries participating in NATO's military structure. Nuclear matters are discussed by the Nuclear Planning Group (NPG).

THE NATO COMMANDS. The strategic area covered by the North Atlantic Treaty is divided among three Commands: Allied Command Europe (ACE), Allied Command Atlantic (ACLANT) and Allied Command Channel (ACCHAN). Plans for the defence of the North American area are developed by the Canada-United States Regional Planning Group (CUSRPG). The main strategic areas are divided into many sub-areas which are too numerous to mention here. Generally, the forces of member countries remain under national command in peacetime; however, some are placed under operational command of control of NATO, some are already assigned to NATO Commands and others are earmarked for these Commands.

THE EUROPEAN COMMAND. Allied Command Europe (ACE) covers the area extending from the North Cape to the Mediterranean and from the Atlantic to the eastern border of Turkey, excluding the United Kingdom and Portugal, the defence of which does not fall under any one NATO Command. ACE is sub-divided into a number of Subordinate Commands and comes under the Supreme Allied Commander Europe (SACEUR) whose headquarters, near Mons in Belgium, are known as SHAPE (Supreme Headquarters Allied Powers Europe).

THE ATLANTIC OCEAN COMMAND. The Allied Command Atlantic covers approximately 12 million square miles of the Atlantic Ocean. This area extends from the North Pole to the Tropic of Cancer and from the coastal waters of North America to the coasts of Europe and Africa, except for the Channel and the British Isles. ACLANT is subdivided into a number of subordinate Commands, and the area comes under the Supreme Allied Commander Atlantic (SACLANT). The Standing Naval Force Atlantic (STANAVFORLANT), made up of ships from NATO navies normally operating in the Atlantic area, is under the direct command of SACLANT.

THE CHANNEL COMMAND. The Allied Command Channel covers the English Channel and the southern areas of the North Sea. Its mission is to protect merchant shipping in the area, co-operating with SACEUR in the air defence of the Channel. The Allied Commander-in-Chief Channel (CINCHAN) has under his orders the NATO Standing Naval Force Channel (STANAVFORCHAN) which is a permanent force comprising mine counter-measures vessels of different NATO countries.

## COMMONLY USED NATO ABBREVIATIONS

| | |
|---|---|
| **ACCHAN** | Allied Command Channel |
| **ACE** | Allied Command Europe |
| **ACLANT** | Allied Command Atlantic |
| **ANCA** | Allied Naval Communications Agency |
| **CINCEASLANT** | Commander-in-Chief Eastern Atlantic Area |
| **CINCHAN** | Commander-in-Chief Channel and Southern North Sea |
| **CINCIBERLANT** | Commander-in-Chief Iberian Atlantic Area |
| **CINCWESTLANT** | Commander-in-Chief Western Atlantic Area |
| **IBERLANT** | Iberian Atlantic Area |
| **NAVOCFORMED** | Navy on-call Force Mediterranean |
| **SACEUR** | Supreme Allied Commander Europe |
| **SACLANT** | Supreme Allied Commander Atlantic |

# RECOGNITION SILHOUETTES

CLEMENCEAU, 'CLEMENCEAU' Class CVA　　　　　Fra (2)

DEDALO, Ex-USA 'INDEPENDENCE' Class CVL　　　　Spn (2)

ENTERPRISE, 'ENTERPRISE' Class CVN　　　　　USA (1)

FORRESTAL, 'FORRESTAL' Class CV　　　　　USA (4)

SARATOGA, 'FORRESTAL' Class CV          USA (4)

'HANCOCK/INTREPID' Class CVA/CV          USA (3)

GIUSEPPE GARIBALDI CVL          Ita (1)

INVINCIBLE, 'INVINCIBLE' Class CHG          UK (2)

ARK ROYAL, 'INVINCIBLE' Class CHG UK (1)

JOHN F. KENNEDY, 'KITTY HAWK' Class CV USA (1)

KITTY HAWK, 'KITTY HAWK' Class CV USA (3)

CORAL SEA, 'MIDWAY' Class CV USA (2)

NIMITZ, 'NIMITZ' Class CVN                    USA (3+3)

VITORIO VENETO CHG                            Ita (1)

PRINCIPE DE ASTURIAS CVL                      Spn (1)

JEANNE D'ARC CVH                              Fra (1)

18

NEW JERSEY, 'IOWA' Class                    USA (4)

BAINBRIDGE, 'BAINBRIDGE' Class CGN          USA (1)

ANDREA DORIA, 'ANDREA DORIA' Class DLG      Ita (2)

WAINWRIGHT, 'BELKNAP' Class CG              USA (9)

CALIFORNIA, 'CALIFORNIA' Class CGN                    USA (2)

LEAHY, 'LEAHY' Class CG                    USA (9)

COLBERT CLG                    Fra (1)

LONG BEACH, 'LONG BEACH' Class CGN                    USA (1)

TICONDEROGA, 'TICONDEROGA' Class CG          USA (4+12)

VIRGINIA, 'VIRGINIA' Class CGN          USA (4)

TRUXTUN, 'TRUXTUN' Class CGN          USA (1)

'ALLEN M. SUMNER (FRAM II)' Class DD, DDG          Gre (1), Tur (1)

AUDACE, 'AUDACE' Class DDG                    Ita (2)

ALCONIT, 'Type C 65' FF                       Fra (1)

BRISTOL, 'Type 82' DLG                        UK (1)

GEORGE LEYGUES, 'Type C 70' (A/S) DDG         Fra (4+2+1)

'CARPENTER (FRAM I)' Class DD                    Tur (2)

LÜTJENS, 'MOD. CHARLES F. ADAMS' Class DDG        GFR (3)

'CHARLES F. ADAMS' Class DDG              USA (23)

FARRAGUT, 'COONTZ' Class DDG             USA (10)

'COUNTY' Class DLGH (Exocet)    UK (2)

DUPERRE, 'Type T 53' (modified ASW) DD    Fra (1)

IROQUOIS, 'DD 280' Class DDH    Can (4)

TOURVILLE, 'Type F 67' DDG    Fra (3)

'FLETCHER' Class DD (4-gun type)  GFR (2), Gre (2), Spn (3)

DECATUR, Converted 'FORREST SHERMAN' and  USA (4)
'HULL' Classes DDG

'FLETCHER' Class DD (5-gun type)  Spn (1)

'FORREST SHERMAN' and 'HULL' Classes  USA (6)
(ASW modified) DD

'GEARING (FRAM I)' Class DD                Gre (6), Spn (5), Tur (6)

HAMBURG, 'HAMBURG' Class DD                GFR (4)

'GEARING (FRAM II)' Class DD                Tur (2)

IMPAVIDO, 'IMPAVIDO' Class DDG                Ita (2)

'KIDD' Class DDG                    USA (4)

SPRUANCE, 'SPRUANCE' Class DD              USA (31)

ROGER DE LAURIA, 'ROGER DE LAURIA' Class DD      Spn (1)

SUFFREN, 'SUFFREN' Class DLG                Fra (2)

'Type 42' DDGH                                    UK (10+2)

'Type 47' DDG                                     Fra (2)

'Type T 47' (ASW) DD                              Fra (4)

LA GALISSIONIERE', 'Type T 56' DDH               Fra (1)

'Type A 69' FFG                                    Fra (17)

ALPINO, 'ALPINO' Class FF                          Ita (2)

'ALMIRANTE PEREIRA DE SILVA' Class FF              Por (2)

AMAZON, 'AMAZON' Class (Type 21) FFG               UK (6)

ANNAPOLIS, 'ANNAPOLIS' Class DDG Can (2)

CARLO BERGAMINI, 'BERGAMINI' Class FF Ita (2)

BALEARES, 'BALEARES' (F 70) Class FFG Spn (5)

BERK, 'BERK' Class FF Tur (2)

30

'BREMEN' Class (Type 122) FF                 GFR (6)

'BRONSTEIN' Class FF                          USA (2)

BROADSWORD, 'BROADSWORD' Class (Type 22) FFGH     UK (6+8)

'BROOKE' Class FFG                            USA (6)

Ex-USA 'CANNON' Class FF                                          Gre (4)

'DESCUBIERTA' Class (F 30) FF                                     Spn (6)

'COMMANDANTE JOAO BELO' Class FF                                  Por (4)

GARCIA, 'GARCIA' Class FF                                         USA (2)

'GARCIA' Class (with LAMPS) FF                    USA (8)

'HVIDBJORNEN' Class FF                    Den (4)

GLOVER, 'GLOVER' Class FF                    USA (1)

'MOD. HVIDBJØRNEN' Class FF                    Den (1)

'JACOB VAN HEEMSKERCK' Class FFG          Neth (2)

DOWNES, 'KNOX' Class FF          USA ( )

JOAO COUTINHO, 'JOAO COUTINHO' Class FF          Por (2)

'KNOX' Class FF (Improved)          USA( )

KÖLN, 'KÖLN' Class FF                              GFR (3), Tur (2)

'LEANDER BROAD BEAM' Class FFGH             UK (4)

'KORTENAER' Class FF                             Neth (10)

'LEANDER' Class FFH (Ikara)                           UK (6)

'LEANDER' Class FFGH (Exocet)　　　　　　　　UK (4)

LUPO, 'LUPO' Class FF　　　　　　　　Ita (4)

'LEANDER Batch 2TA' Class FFGH　　　　　　　　UK (4)

MACKENZIE, 'MACKENZIE' Class DD　　　　　　　　Can (4)

MAESTRALE, 'MAESTRALE' Class — Ita (8)

'OLIVER HAZARD PERRY' Class FFG — USA (42+9+(1))

'NIELS JUEL' Class FF — Den (3)

OSLO, 'OSLO' Class F/FFG — Nor (5)

PEDER SKRAM, 'PEDER SKRAM' Class FF          Den (2)

GATINEAU, 'IMPROVED RESTIGOUCHE' Class DD          Can (4)

CHAUDIERE, 'RESTIGOUCHE' Class DD          Can (3)

'MOD. ROTHESAY' Class FFH          UK (4)

SAGUENAY, 'ST. LAURENT' Class DDH                    Can (6)

'VAN SPEIJK' Class FF                    Neth (6)

TROMP, 'TROMP' Class DDGH                    Neth (2)

'WIELINGEN' Class (E-71) FF                    Blg (4)

ALBATROS, 'ALBATROS' Class PF Ita (4)

'SLEIPNER' Class FF Nor (2)

PIETRO DE CRISTOFARO, 'PIETRO DE CRISOFARO' Class PF Ita (4)

'THETIS' Class (Type 420) PF GFR (5)

IWO JIMA, 'IWO JIMA', Class LPH                    USA (7)

TARAWA, 'TARAWA' Class LHA                    USA (5)

## GLOSSARY

| | |
|---|---|
| **AA** | Anti-aircraft |
| **AAW** | Anti-aircraft warfare |
| **ADS** | Automatic defence system |
| **A/S, ASW** | Anti-submarine warfare |
| **ASROC** | Anti-submarine rocket |
| **BPDMS** | Basic point defence missile system |
| **CC** | Cruiser |
| **CG** | Cruiser, guided missile (including surface to air missiles) |
| **CGN** | Cruiser, guided missile, nuclear powered |
| **CHG** | Helicopter cruiser, guided missile |
| **CIWS** | Close-in weapon system |
| **CL** | Cruiser, light |
| **CLG** | Cruiser, light, guided missile |
| **CODAG, CODOG, COGAG, COGOG, COSAG** | Abbreviations of mixed propulsion systems: combined diesel and gas turbine; diesel or gas turbine; gas turbine and gas turbine; gas turbine or gas turbine; steam and gas turbine |
| **CV** | Aircraft carrier |
| **CVA** | Aircraft carrier, attack |
| **CVH** | Aircraft carrier, helicopter |
| **CVGH** | Aircraft carrier, helicopter, guided missile |
| **CVL** | Aircraft carrier, light |
| **CVN** | Aircraft carrier, nuclear-powered |
| **DC** | Depth charge |
| **DCT** | Depth charge thrower |
| **DD** | Destroyer |
| **DDG** | Destroyer, guided missile |
| **DDGH** | Destroyer, guided missile, anti-submarine helicopter |
| **DDH** | Destroyer, anti-submarine helicopter |
| **DLG** | Destroyer, light, guided missile (US) |
| **DLGH** | Destroyer, light, guided missile, anti-submarine helicopter (US) |
| **Displacement** | Basically the weight of water displaced by a ship's hull when floating: <br> a) Light: without fuel, water or ammunition <br> b) Standard: fully manned and stored but without fuel or reserve feed water <br> c) Full load: fully laden with all stores, ammunition, fuel and water |
| **DP** | Dual purpose (gun) for surface or AA use |
| **FF** | Frigate |
| **FFG** | Frigate, guided missile |
| **F/FFG** | Frigate, Fleet, guided missile |
| **FFGH** | Frigate, guided missile, anti-submarine helicopter |
| **FFH** | Frigate, anti-submarine helicopter |
| **FRAM** | Fleet Rehabilitation and Modernisation Programme (USA) |

**Horsepower**    Power developed or applied:

a) bhp: brake horse power = power available at crankshaft

b) shp: shaft horse power = power delivered to the propeller shaft

c) ihp: indicated horse power = power produced by expansion of gases in the cylinders of reciprocating steam engines

**Length**    Expressed in various ways:

a) oa: overall = length between extremities

b) pp: between perpendiculars = between fore side of the stem and after side of rudderpost

c) wl: water-line = between extremities on the water-line

**LHA**    Amphibious support ship

| | |
|---|---|
| **LPH** | Amphibious assault ship (US); Landing ship, personnel and helicopters (UK) |
| **NBC** | Nuclear, biological and chemical (warfare) |
| **n miles** | Nautical miles (Imperial) |
| **NTDS** | Naval tactical data system |
| **PDMS** | Point defence missile system |
| **PF** | Patrol escort (US) |
| **SAM** | Surface to air missile |
| **SLBM** | Submarine launched ballistic missile |
| **SNLE** | Nuclear-powered ballistic missile submarine (French) |
| **SS** | Attack submarine |
| **SSB** | Ballistic missile submarine |
| **SSBN** | Nuclear-powered ballistic missile submarine |
| **SSG** | Guided missile submarine |
| **SSN** | Nuclear-powered attack submarine |

# Reference Section

## FRANCE

| | |
|---|---|
| **AGOSTA** | S 620 |
| **BÉVEZIERS** | S 621 |
| **LA PRAYA** | S 622 |
| **OUESSANT** | S 623 |

## SPAIN ('S 70' CLASS - Spanish built)

| | |
|---|---|
| **GALERNA** | S 71 |
| **SIROCO** | S 72 |
| **MISTRAL** | S 73 |
| **TRAMONTANA** | S 74 |

*Agosta class ("Beveziers") 11/1981*
*(Dr. Giorgio Arra)*

**Displacement, tons:** 1 200 standard; 1 450 surfaced; 1 725 dived
**Dimensions, feet (metres):** 221.7 × 22.3 × 17.7 *(67.6 × 6.8 × 5.4)*
**Torpedo tubes:** 4—21 in *(533 mm)* (bow) (20 torpedoes)
**Main machinery:** Diesel-electric; 2 SEMT-Pielstick 16 PA4 diesels 3 600 hp; 1 main motor (3 500 kW) 4 600 hp; 1 cruising motor (23 kW); 1 shaft
**Speed, knots:** 12 surfaced; 20 dived
**Range, miles:** 8 500 at 9 knots (snorting); 350 at 3.5 knots (dived)
**Endurance:** 45 days
**Complement:** 52 (7 officers, 45 men)
**Commissioned:** 1977-78

## FRANCE

Building of this class was announced in 1970 under the third five-year new construction plan 1971-75.

**Missiles:** All are to be armed with SM-39 Exocet.

## SPAIN

**Commissioned:** 1983-86

First two ordered 9 May 1975 and second pair 29 June 1977. Building with some French advice. About 67 per cent of equipment and structure from Spanish sources.

| BARBEL | SS 580 |
| BLUEBACK | SS 581 |
| BONEFISH | SS 582 |

**Displacement, tons:** 2 145 surfaced; 2 894 dived
**Dimensions, feet (metres):** 219.1 × 29 × 28 *(66.8 × 8.8 × 8.5)*
**Torpedo tubes:** 6—21 in *(533 mm)* bow (Mk 58)
**Main machinery:** 3 diesels (Fairbanks-Morse); 4 800 bhp; 2 electric motors (General Electric); 3 150 shp; 1 shaft
**Speed, knots:** 15 surfaced; 21 dived
**Complement:** 85 (8 officers, 77 men)
**Commissioned:** 1959

These submarines were the last non-nuclear combatant submarines built by the US Navy. All three were authorised in the FY 1956 new construction programme.

*Barbel* homeported at Sasebo, Japan.

**Construction:** *Blueback* was the first submarine built by the Ingalls Shipbuilding Corp at Pascagoula, Mississippi, and *Bonefish* was the first constructed at the New York Shipbuilding Corp yard in Camden, New Jersey.

**Design:** These submarines have the 'tear drop' hull design which was tested in the experimental submarine *Albacore*. As built, their fore planes were bow-mounted; subsequently moved to the sail.

*Barbel class ("Blueback") 6 / 1985 (Dr. Giorgio Arra)*

| | |
|---|---|
| LAFAYETTE | SSBN 616 |
| ALEXANDER HAMILTON | SSBN 617 |
| ANDREW JACKSON | SSBN 619 |
| JOHN ADAMS | SSBN 620 |
| JAMES MONROE | SSBN 622 |
| NATHAN HALE | SSBN 623 |
| WOODROW WILSON | SSBN 624 |
| HENRY CLAY | SSBN 625 |
| DANIEL WEBSTER | SSBN 626 |
| JAMES MADISON* | SSBN 627 |
| TECUMSEH | SSBN 628 |
| DANIEL BOONE* | SSBN 629 |
| JOHN C. CALHOUN* | SSBN 630 |
| ULYSSES S. GRANT | SSBN 631 |
| VON STEUBEN* | SSBN 632 |
| CASIMIR PULASKI* | SSBN 633 |
| STONEWALL JACKSON* | SSBN 634 |
| SAM RAYBURN | SSBN 635 |
| NATHANAEL GREENE | SSBN 636 |
| BENJAMIN FRANKLIN* | SSBN 640 |
| SIMON BOLIVAR* | SSBN 641 |
| KAMEHAMEHA | SSBN 642 |
| GEORGE BANCROFT* | SSBN 643 |
| LEWIS AND CLARK | SSBN 644 |
| JAMES K. POLK | SSBN 645 |
| GEORGE C. MARSHALL | SSBN 654 |
| HENRY L. STIMSON* | SSBN 655 |
| GEORGE WASHINGTON CARVER | SSBN 656 |
| FRANCIS SCOTT KEY* | SSBN 657 |
| MARIANO G. VALLEJO* | SSBN 658 |
| WILL ROGERS | SSBN 659 |

\* = Trident modified

*Benjamin Franklin/Lafayette classes
("George C. Marshall") 1985
(Dr. Giorgio Arra)*

**Displacement, tons:** 6 650 light surfaced; 7 250 standard surfaced; 8 250 dived
**Dimensions, feet (metres):** 425 × 33 × 31.5 *(129.5 × 10.1 × 9.6)*
**Missiles:** 16 tubes for Poseidon C-3 or Trident SLBM (see *Missile* notes)
**Torpedo tubes:** 4—21 in *(533 mm)* Mk 65 (bow)
**Main machinery:** 1 pressurised-water cooled S5W (Westinghouse) reactor; 2 geared turbines; 15 000 shp; 1 shaft
**Speed, knots:** 20 surfaced; approx 30 dived
**Complement:** 159 (15 officers, 144 enlisted men)
**Commissioned:** 1963-67

**Engineering:** *Benjamin Franklin* and subsequent submarines of this class have been fitted with quieter machinery and are considered as a separate class. All SSBNs have diesel-electric stand-by machinery, snorts, and 'outboard' auxiliary propeller for emergency use.

**Missiles: Polaris;** The first eight submarines of this class were fitted with the Polaris A-2 missile (1 500 n mile range) and the next 23 with the Polaris A-3 missile (2 500 n mile range).

**Poseidon (C-3);** *James Madison* was the first submarine to undergo conversion to carry the Poseidon missile.
**Trident I (C-4);** Between 24 September 1978 and 10 December 1982 twelve of this class were converted to launch Trident I missiles.

## FRANCE

| | |
|---|---|
| **DAPHNÉ** | S 641 |
| **DIANE** | S 642 |
| **DORIS** | S 643 |
| **FLORE** | S 645 |
| **GALATÉE** | S 646 |
| **JUNON** | S 648 |
| **VENUS** | S 649 |
| **PSYCHÉ** | S 650 |
| **SIRÈNE** | S 651 |

## PORTUGAL

| | |
|---|---|
| **ALBACORA** | S 163 |
| **BARRACUDA** | S 164 |
| **DELFIM** | S 166 |

## SPAIN ('S 60' CLASS)

| | |
|---|---|
| **DELFIN** | S 61 |
| **TONINA** | S 62 |
| **MARSOPA** | S 63 |
| **NARVAL** | S 64 |

*Daphne class ("Diane") 10/1985
(Maritime Photographic)*

**Displacement, tons:** 860 surfaced; 1 038 dived
**Dimensions, feet (metres):** 189.6 × 22.3 × 15.1 *(57.8 × 6.8 × 4.6)*
**Torpedo tubes:** 12—21.7 in *(550 mm)* (8 bow, 4 stern)
**Main machinery:** SEMT-Pielstick diesel-electric; 2 diesels; 1 224 bhp; 2 electric motors; 2 600 bhp; 2 shafts
**Range, miles:** 2 700 at 12.5 knots (surfaced); 10 000 at 7 knots (surfaced); 4 500 at 5 knots (snorting); 3 000 at 7 knots (snorting)
**Speed, knots:** 13.5 surfaced; 16 dived
**Complement:** 45 (6 officers, 39 men)
**Commissioned:** 1964-70

## PORTUGAL

**Commissioned:** 1967-69

Basically similar to the French 'Daphne' type but slightly modified to suit Portuguese requirements.

## SPAIN

**Commissioned:** 1973-75

Identical to the French 'Daphne' class and built with extensive French assistance.

DARTER                                    SS 576

**Displacement, tons:** 1 720 surfaced; 2 388 dived
**Dimensions, feet (metres):** 284.5 × 27.2 × 19
  *(86.7 × 8.3 × 5.8)*
**Torpedo tubes:** 8—21 in *(533 mm)* 6 bow; 2
  stern
**Main machinery:** 3 diesels (Fairbanks-Morse);
  4 500 bhp; 2 electric motors (Elliott); 5 500 shp;
  2 shafts
**Speed, knots:** 19.5 surfaced; 14 dived
**Complement:** 93 (8 officers, 85 men)
**Commissioned:** 1956

Authorised in the FY 1954 shipbuilding
programme. No additional submarines of this
type were built because of shift to high-speed hull
design and nuclear propulsion.
  Homeport shifted to Sasebo, Japan in March
1979.

*Darter class ("Darter") 1 / 1980*
*(Dr. Giorgio Arra)*

**SPAEKHUGGEREN**                          S 327
**SPRINGEREN**                             S 329

**Displacement, tons:** 595 surfaced; 643 dived
**Dimensions, feet (metres):** 177.2 × 15.4 × 13.8
  *(54 × 4.7 × 4.2)*
**Torpedo tubes:** 4—21 in *(533 mm)*
**Main machinery:** 2 Burmeister & Wain 12-cyl
  diesels; 1 200 bhp; 2 electric motors; 1 200 hp
**Speed, knots:** 16 surfaced and dived
**Range, miles:** 4 000 at 8 knots
**Complement:** 31
**Commissioned:** 1959-64

Active and passive sonar. Now reaching the end
of their hull lives.

*Delfinen class (*Royal Danish Navy*)*

**DOLPHIN** AGSS 555

**Displacement, tons:** 800 standard; 930 full load
**Dimensions, feet (metres):** 152 × 19.3 × 18 *(46.3 × 5.9 × 5.5)*
**Torpedo tubes:** Removed
**Main machinery:** Diesel-electric (2 Detroit 12 V71 diesels); 1 650 hp; 1 shaft
**Speed, knots:** 15+ dived
**Complement:** 22 (7 officers, 15 enlisted men) plus 4 to 7 scientists
**Commissioned:** 1968

Specifically designed for deep-diving operations. Authorised in the FY 1961 new construction programme but delayed because of changes in mission and equipment coupled with higher priorities being given to other submarine projects. Fitted for deep-ocean sonar and oceanographic research. She is highly automated and has three computer-operated systems, a safety system, hovering system, and one that is classified. The digital-computer submarine safety system monitors equipment and provides data on closed-circuit television screens; malfunctions in equipment set off an alarm and if they are not corrected within the prescribed time the system, unless overridden by an operator, automatically brings the submarine to the surface. There are several research stations for scientists and she is fitted to take water samples down to her operating depth.

Underwater endurance is limited (endurance and habitability were considered of secondary importance in design).

**Design:** No conventional hydroplanes are mounted, improved rudder design and other features provide manoeuvring control and hovering capability.

*Dolphin class ("Dolphin") 7/1969 (US Navy)*

| | |
|---|---|
| **SAM HOUSTON** | SSN 609 |
| **JOHN MARSHALL** | SSN 611 |

**Displacement, tons:** 6 955 surfaced; 7 880 dived
**Dimensions, feet (metres):** 410 × 33 × 32 *(125 × 10.1 × 9.8)*
**Torpedo tubes:** 4—21 in *(533 mm)* bow
**Main machinery:** 1 pressurised-water cooled S5W (Westinghouse) reactor; 2 geared turbines (General Electric); 15 000 shp; 1 shaft
**Speed, knots:** 20 surfaced; 30 dived
**Complement:** 143 (13 officers, 130 enlisted men)
**Commissioned:** 1962

These submarines were designed specifically for the ballistic missile role and were larger and better arranged than the earlier 'George Washington' class submarines. This class was first authorised in the FY 1959 programme. These submarines and the previous 'George Washington' class were not converted to carry the Poseidon missile because of material limitations and the age they would be after conversion.

In the FY 1981 budget, funds were included to remove this class from the SLBM force and convert them to SSNs. The conversion includes decommissioning the missile section, putting cement blocks in the missile tubes as ballast compensation and removing one of the SINS navigation systems and the missile fire control systems. Conversion of each submarine costs an estimated $400 000. *Thomas A. Edison* was

*Ethan Allen class, 9/1977*
*(US Navy)*

decommissioned 1 December 1983 at Bremerton after the removal of her missile compartment and then laid up. *Thomas Jefferson* followed on 1 February 1985.

**Conversion:** SSN 609 and 611 have been modified as 'Amphibious Transports' at Puget Sound Naval Shipyard, September 1983-September 1985. This included additional troop berthing, removal of some missile tube bases, conversion of others as air-locks and stowage for equipment. Life expectancy, late 1990s.

**Designation:** SSBN 609 reclassified as SSN on 10 November 1980. SSBN 611 reclassified as SSN on 1 May 1981.

**GLENARD P. LIPSCOMB**   SSN 685

**Displacement, tons:** 5 813 standard; 6 480 dived
**Dimensions, feet (metres):** 365 × 31.7 × 31
 *(111.3 × 9.7 × 9.5)*
**Missiles:** 4 Harpoon; to be fitted for 8 Tomahawk
**Torpedo tubes:** 4—21 in *(533 mm)* amidships
**A/S weapons:** SUBROC and A/S torpedoes
**Main machinery:** 1 pressurised-water cooled
 S5Wa (Westinghouse) reactor; turbine-electric
 drive (General Electric); 1 shaft
**Speed, knots:** approx 25+ dived
**Complement:** 141 (13 officers, 128 enlisted
 men)
**Commissioned:** 1974

Studies of a specifically 'quiet' submarine were
begun in October 1964. After certain setbacks
approval for the construction of this submarine
was announced on 25 October 1968 and the
contract awarded to General Dynamics on 14
October 1970.

The Turbine-Electric Drive Submarine (TEDS)
was constructed to test 'a combination of
advanced silencing techniques' involving 'a new
kind of propulsion system, and new and quieter
machinery of various kinds', according to the
Department of Defense. TEDS eliminates the
noisy reduction gears of standard steam turbine
power plants. The turbine-electric power plant is
larger and heavier than comparable geared
steam turbine submarine machinery. *Tullibee*
(SSN 597) was an earlier effort at noise reduction
through a turbine-electric nuclear plant.

No further class of turbine-electric nuclear
submarines has been proposed. Rather, quieting
features developed in *Glenard P. Lipscomb* which
do not detract from speed have been incorporated
in the 'Los Angeles' design.

*Glenard P. Lipscomb class ("Glenard
P. Lipscomb") 7/1980 (*L & L van
Ginderen*)*

## TURKEY

**BURAKREIS** (Ex-USS *Seafox*)            S 335
**MURATREIS** (Ex-USS *Razorback*)          S 336
**ORUÇREIS** (Ex-USS *Pomfret*)             S 337
**ULUÇALIREIS** (Ex-USS *Thornback*)        S 338
**ÇERBE** (Ex-USS *Trutta*)                 S 340
**PREVEZE** (Ex-USS *Entemedor*)            S 345
**BIRINCI INÖNÜ** (Ex-USS *Threadfin*)      S 346

## GREECE

**PAPANIKOLIS** (ex-USS *Hardhead*)         S 114

**Displacement, tons:** 1 848 surfaced; 2 440 dived
**Dimensions, feet (metres):** 306 × 27 × 17 *(93.2 × 8.2 × 5.2)*
**Torpedo tubes:** 10—21 in *(533 mm)* (6 bow, 4 stern); (24 torpedoes or 40 mines carried)
**Main machinery:** 3 General Motors diesels; 4 800 hp; 2 electric motors; 5 400 hp
**Speed, knots:** 17 surfaced; 14-15 dived
**Range, miles:** 12 000 at 10 knots surfaced
**Complement:** 82
**Commissioned:** 1944-45

## TURKEY

**Transfers:** *Burakreis* December 1970, *Muratreis* 17 November 1970, *Oruçeis* 3 May 1972, *Çerbe* June 1972, *Preveze, Uluçalireis* 24 August 1973, *Birinci Inönü* 15 August 1973.

## GREECE

**Complement:** 84
**Commissioned:** 1944
Transferred 26 July 1972 by sale. Training boat.

*Guppy IIA class ("Murat Reis")*
*3/1982 (Selim Sam)*

## GREECE

**KATSONIS** (ex-USS *Remora*)   S 115

## TURKEY

**CANAKKALE** (ex-USS *Cobbler*)   S 341
**IKINCI INONÜ** (ex-USS *Corporal*)   S 333

**Displacement, tons:** 1 975 standard; 2 450 dived
**Dimensions, feet (metres):** 326.5 × 27 × 17 *(99.4 × 8.2 × 5.2)*
**Torpedo tubes:** 10—21 in *(533 mm)* (6 bow, 4 stern)
**Main machinery:** 4 diesels; 6 400 hp; 2 electric motors; 5 400 shp; 2 shafts
**Speed, knots:** 20 surfaced; 15 dived
**Range, miles:** 12 000 at 10 knots (surfaced)
**Complement:** 85
**Commissioned:** 1946

Originally of the wartime 'Tench' class, subsequently converted under the 'Guppy II' programme and, in 1961-62, to 'Guppy III'. Among other modifications this involved the fitting of BQG-4 sonar (PUFFS) for dived fire control, in addition to the BQR-2 array sonar. Transferred 29 October 1973 by sale. Training boat.

### GREECE

Transferred 29 October 1973 by sale. Training boat.

### TURKEY

**Commissioned:** 1945
Transferred 21 November 1973.

*Guppy III class ("Canakkale") 1979
(Selçuk Emre)*

**GYMNOTE**                      S 655

**Displacement, tonnes:** 3 340 surfaced; 3 870 dived
**Dimensions, feet (metres):** 274.9 × 35.8 × 25.3 *(83.8 × 10.9 × 7.7)*
**Missile launchers:** 2 tubes for MSBS
**Main machinery:** 4 sets 620 kW diesel-electric; 2 electric motors; 2 600 hp; 2 shafts
**Speed, knots:** 11 surfaced; 10 dived
**Range, miles:** 5 500 at 7 knots
**Complement:** 78 (8 officers, 70 men)
**Commissioned:** 1966

An experimental submarine for testing ballistic missiles for the French nuclear-powered SSBNs, and for use as an underwater laboratory to prove equipment and arms for nuclear-powered submarines.

Started conversion in early 1977 (completion January 1979) for trial firings of M-4 missiles. First M-4 trials from land November 1980. Further refit in 1980 to prepare for new M-4 trials in 1981—first M-4 fired 10 March 1982. To reserve in June 1986.

*Gymnote, 1981 (*G. Koop*)*

| LE FOUDROYANT | S 610 |
| LE REDOUTABLE | S 611 |
| LE TERRIBLE | S 612 |
| L'INDOMPTABLE | S 613 |
| LE TONNANT | S 614 |

**Displacement, tons:** 8 045 surfaced; 8 940 dived
**Dimensions, feet (metres):** 422.1 × 34.8 × 32.8
  *(128.7 × 10.6 × 10)*
**Missiles:** 16 tubes amidships for MSBS M-20
**Torpedo tubes:** 4—21 in *(533 mm)* (18
  torpedoes)
**Nuclear reactor:** 1 pressurised water-cooled
**Main machinery:** 2 steam turbines; 2 turbo-
  alternators; 1 electric motor; 16 000 hp; 1 shaft
**Auxiliary propulsion:** Twin diesel; 1 306 hp; fuel
  for 5 000 miles
**Speed, knots:** 20+ surfaced; 25 dived
**Complement:** 2 alternating crews each of 135
  (15 officers, 120 men)
**Commissioned:** 1974-80

*Le Redoutable* was the first French nuclear-
powered, ballistic missile armed submarine and
the prototype of the *'Force de Dissuasion'*.
   The plan is to have four boats operational and
one in refit

**Missiles:** Originally armed with MSBS M-1 of 18
tons launch weight. Subsequently MSBS M-2 of
19.9 tons with a 1 300 n. mile range and a 500 kt
head was shipped, the first submarine with this
outfit being *Le Redoutable* at her 1976 refit. The
1 500 n. mile M-20 missiles with a megaton
reinforced head have now been shipped in all
submarines. All except *Le Redoutable* will be
fitted with M-4 missiles in the following order—
*Le Tonnant, Le Terrible, Le Foudroyant,
L'Indomptable.* The order of refits reported as
*Tonnant, L'Indomptable, Terrible* and *Foudroyant*.
M-4 has six 150 kt MIRV heads and a range of
2 500-3 000 n. miles. *Le Tonnant* started a three
year refit in February 1985 to fit her for M-4/TN-
71 which has a range of more than 3 125 miles
*(5 000 km)*.
   SM 39 will be carried in SNLEs in due course.

*Le Redoutable class ("Le
Foudroyant") 1981 (French Navy)*

**L'INFLEXIBLE** S 615

**Displacement, tons:** 8 080 surfaced; 8 920 dived
**Dimensions, feet (metres):** 422.1 × 34.8 × 32.8
*(128.7 × 10.6 × 10)*
**Missiles:** 16 tubes for M-4/TN-70
**Torpedo tubes:** 4—21 in *(533 mm)* for L5 and L7
torpedoes or SM 39 missiles (18 torpedoes)
**Nuclear reactor:** 1 pressurised water-cooled
**Main machinery:** 2 steam turbines; 2 turbo
alternators; 1 electric motor; 16 000 hp; 1 shaft
**Auxiliary propulsion:** Diesel-electric for 5 000
miles
**Speed, knots:** 25 dived
**Complement:** 2 alternating crews each of 127
(15 officers, 44 senior and 68 junior ratings)
**Commissioned:** 1985

In September 1978 a decision was taken by
President Giscard D'Estaing to proceed with the
construction of a sixth SNLE to be of an
intermediate type between her predecessors and
a new class planned for 1990-2000. Ordered 26
November 1978. Her cost will be about 2 000
million francs. The reasoning behind this order is
that in order to have three submarines
continuously available, of which two are on
patrol, six hulls are required. If the ordering of
this boat had not been delayed in December 1975
she would have been built with the M-20 missile
system instead of the M-4 system which will be
operational in 1985. Having accepted that France
would need six SNLE operational by 2000 the
logic of having the most up-to-date missile
system is clear. The M-4 with a range of some
2 500-3 000 miles and carrying six 150 kt MIRV
heads will combine with improved inertial
navigation systems, sonar, diving depth, reactor
and armament to provide a submarine 'qui
utilisera les techniques des années 80' as M.
Bourges (late Minister of Defence) described it.
Commissionned 1 April 1985.

*L'Inflexible (Jean Biaugeaud)*

| | |
|---|---|
| LOS ANGELES | SSN 688 |
| BATON ROUGE | SSN 689 |
| PHILADELPHIA | SSN 690 |
| MEMPHIS | SSN 691 |
| OMAHA | SSN 692 |
| CINCINNATI | SSN 693 |
| GROTON | SSN 694 |
| BIRMINGHAM | SSN 695 |
| NEW YORK CITY | SSN 696 |
| INDIANAPOLIS | SSN 697 |
| BREMERTON | SSN 698 |
| JACKSONVILLE | SSN 699 |
| DALLAS | SSN 700 |
| LA JOLLA | SSN 701 |
| PHOENIX | SSN 702 |
| BOSTON | SSN 703 |
| BALTIMORE | SSN 704 |
| CITY OF CORPUS CHRISTI | SSN 705 |
| ALBUQUERQUE | SSN 706 |
| PORTSMOUTH | SSN 707 |
| MINNEAPOLIS-SAINT PAUL | SSN 708 |
| HYMAN G. RICKOVER | SSN 709 |
| AUGUSTA | SSN 710 |
| SAN FRANCISCO | SSN 711 |
| ATLANTA | SSN 712 |
| HOUSTON | SSN 713 |
| NORFOLK | SSN 714 |
| BUFFALO | SSN 715 |
| SALT LAKE CITY | SSN 716 |
| OLYMPIA | SSN 717 |
| HONOLULU | SSN 718 |
| PROVIDENCE | SSN 719 |
| PITTSBURGH | SSN 720 |
| CHICAGO | SSN 721 |
| KEYWEST | SSN 722 |
| OKLAHOMA CITY | SSN 723 |
| LOUISVILLE | SSN 724 |
| HELENA | SSN 725 |
| NEWPORT NEWS | SSN 750 |

**Displacement, tons:** 6 000 standard; 6 927 dived
**Dimensions, feet (metres):** 360 × 33 × 32.3
  *(109.7 × 10.1 × 9.9)*
**Missiles:** Tube launched Harpoon (4); Tomahawk
  (8) to be fitted (see *Missiles* note)
**Torpedo tubes:** 4—21 in *(533 mm)* amidships
**A/S weapons:** SUBROC (688-699) and Mk 48
  A/S torpedoes
**Mines:** Can lay mines
**Main machinery:** 1 pressurised-water cooled
  S6G (GE) reactor; 2 geared turbines; 1 shaft;
  approx 35 000 shp
**Speed, knots:** 30+ dived
**Complement:** 142 (13 officers, 129 enlisted
  men)
**Commissioned:** 1986-87 (plus 13 on order or
  building)

**Missiles:** Tomahawk missiles fitted in SSN 703,
704, 712 and 713. SSN 688-718 will carry 12 as
part of the torpedo load. From SSN 719 onwards
15 VLS tubes are being fitted in the bow between
the inner and outer hulls giving each submarine a
15 missile capacity.

*Los Angeles class ("Buffalo")*
*8/1985 (*Dr. Giorgio Arra*)*

| NARHVALEN | S 320 |
| NORDKAPEREN | S 321 |

**Displacement, tons:** 420 surfaced; 450 dived
**Dimensions, feet (metres):** 145.3 × 15 × 13.8
  *(44.3 × 4.6 × 4.2)*
**Torpedo tubes:** 8—21 in *(533 mm)* bow
**Main machinery:** 2 MB diesels; 1 500 bhp; 1
  electric motor; 1 500 bhp
**Speed, knots:** 12 surfaced; 17 dived
**Complement:** 21
**Commissioned:** 1970

These coastal submarines are similar to the West German Improved Type 205 and were built under licence at the Royal Dockyard, Copenhagen with modifications for Danish needs. Active and passive sonar.

*Narhvalen class ("Nordkaperen")*
*(Royal Danish Navy)*

**DAUPHIN** (research)                     S 633
**MORSE**                                  S 638

**Displacement, tons:** 1 320 standard; 1 635
    surfaced; 1 910 dived
**Dimensions, feet (metres):** 255.8 × 23.6 × 18 *(78
    × 7.2 × 5.5)*
**Torpedo tubes:** 6—21.7 in *(550 mm)* bow; 14
    reload torpedoes; capable of minelaying
**Main machinery:** Diesel-electric, three 12-cyl
    SEMT- Pielstick diesels; two 2 400 hp electric
    motors; 2 shafts
**Speed, knots:** 15 surfaced; 18 dived
**Range, miles:** 15 000 at 8 knots (snorting)
**Endurance:** 45 days
**Complement:** 63 (7 officers, 56 men)
**Commissioned:** 1958-60

Improved version based on the West German
Type XXI.

**Deletions:** *Morse* to be deleted in late 1986.

**Reconstruction:** During a five-year
reconstruction programme, announced in 1965
and completed by the end of 1970, these
submarines were given new weapon and
detection equipment at Lorient.

*Narval class ("Dauphin") 9/1981
(Dr. Giorgio Arra)*

**NARWHAL**                    SSN 671

**Displacement, tons:** 4 450 standard; 5 350 dived
**Dimensions, feet (metres):** 314.6 × 37.7 × 27
  *(95.9 × 11.5 × 8.2)*
**Missiles:** 4 Harpoon; to be fitted for 8 Tomahawk
**Torpedo tubes:** 4—21 in *(533 mm)* amidships
**A/S weapons:** A/S torpedoes
**Main machinery:** 1 pressurised water-cooled
  S5G (General Electric) reactor; 2 steam
  turbines; 17 000 shp; 1 shaft
**Speed, knots:** 20+ surfaced; 30+ dived
**Complement:** 141 (13 officers, 128 enlisted
  men)
**Commissioned:** 1969

Authorised in the FY 1964 new construction
programme.

**Design:** *Narwhal* is similar to the 'Sturgeon' class
submarines in hull design.

*Narwhal class ("Narwhal") 1982*
*(Dr. Giorgio Arra)*

## UK

| | |
|---|---|
| OBERON | S 09 |
| ODIN | S 10 |
| ORPHEUS | S 11 |
| OLYMPUS | S 12 |
| OSIRIS | S 13 |
| ONSLAUGHT | S 14 |
| OTTER | S 15 |
| ORACLE | S 16 |
| OCELOT | S 17 |
| OTUS | S 18 |
| OPOSSUM | S 19 |
| OPPORTUNE | S 20 |
| ONYX | S 21 |

'PORPOISE' class:

| | |
|---|---|
| SEALION | S07 |
| WALRUS | S08 |

## CANADA

| | |
|---|---|
| OJIBWA (ex-*Onyx*) | 72 |
| ONONDAGA | 73 |
| OKANAGAN | 74 |

*Oberon/Porpoise classes*
*("Onslaught") 2/1982 (*Michael D. J.
Lennon*)*

**Displacement, tons:** 1 610 standard; 2 030 surfaced; 2 410 dived
**Dimensions, feet (metres):** 295.2 × 26.5 × 18 *(90 × 8.1 × 5.5)*
**Torpedo tubes:** 8—21 in *(533 mm)* (6 bow, 2 stern A/S); 24 torpedoes carried
**Main machinery:** 2 Admiralty Standard Range 1, 16 VMS diesels; 3 680 bhp; 2 electric motors; 6 000 shp; 2 shafts
**Speed, knots:** 12 surfaced; 17 dived
**Range, miles:** 9 000 surfaced
**Complement:** 69 (7 officers, 62 men) in 'Oberon' class; 71 (6 officers, 65 men) in 'Porpoise' class
**Commissioned:** 1961-67

**Deletions:** *Orpheus* and *Oberon* to pay off in 1986—*Sealion* and *Walrus* in 1987.

**Modification:** *Oberon* has been modified with deeper casing to house equipment for the initial training of personnel for nuclear powered submarines. Others of this class are currently undergoing modification.

## CANADA

In 1962 the Ministry of National Defence announced that Canada was to buy three 'Oberon' class submarines in the UK. The first of these patrol submarines was obtained by the Canadian Government from the Royal Navy construction programme. She was laid down as *Onyx* but launched as *Ojibwa*. The other two were Canadian orders. There were some design changes to meet specific new needs including installation of RCN communications equipment and increase of air-conditioning capacity to meet the wide extremes of climate encountered in Canadian operating areas.

| | |
|---|---|
| **OHIO** | SSBN 726 |
| **MICHIGAN** | SSBN 727 |
| **FLORIDA** | SSBN 728 |
| **GEORGIA** | SSBN 729 |
| **HENRY M. JACKSON** | SSBN 730 |
| **ALABAMA** | SSBN 731 |
| **ALASKA** | SSBN 732 |
| **NEVADA** | SSBN 733 |

**Displacement, tons:** 16 600 surfaced; 18 700 dived
**Dimensions, feet (metres):** 560 × 42 × 35.5 *(170.7 × 12.8 × 10.8)*
**Missiles:** 24 tubes for Trident I Submarine-Launched Ballistic Missile (SLBM)
**Torpedo tubes:** 4—21 in *(533 mm)* Mk 68 (bow)
**Main machinery:** 1 pressurised-water cooled S8G (General Electric) reactor; 2 geared turbines; 1 shaft; 60 000 shp
**Speed, knots:** 20+
**Complement:** 171 (16 officers, 155 enlisted men)
**Commissioned:** 1981-86 (plus 9 more building, ordered or projected)

The lead submarine was contracted to the Electric Boat Division of the General Dynamics Corp (Groton, Connecticut) on 25 July 1974. No other US shipyard is currently building submarines of this class, although Newport News Shipbuilding is vastly enlarging its submarine construction capability and has accepted an SSBN refit and may take part in the SSBN building programme in the future.

**Design:** The size of the Trident submarine is dictated primarily by the larger size missile required for 4 or 6 000 mile range and the larger reactor plant to drive the ship. The submarines have 24 tubes in a vertical position.
The principal characteristics of the Trident concept as proposed were: (1) long-range missile (eventually of 6 000 miles (Trident II)) to permit targeting the Soviet Union while the submarine cruises in remote areas, making effective ASW virtually impossible for the foreseeable future, (2) extremely quiet submarines, (3) a high at-sea to in-port ratio.

*Ohio class ("Henry M. Jackson")*
*6/1985 (*Dr. Giorgio Arra*)*

| | |
|---|---|
| PERMIT | SSN 594 |
| PLUNGER | SSN 595 |
| BARB | SSN 596 |
| POLLACK | SSN 603 |
| HADDO | SSN 604 |
| JACK | SSN 605 |
| TINOSA | SSN 606 |
| DACE | SSN 607 |
| GUARDFISH | SSN 612 |
| FLASHER | SSN 613 |
| GREENLING | SSN 614 |
| GATO | SSN 615 |
| HADDOCK | SSN 621 |

**Displacement, tons:** 3 750 standard; *Flasher, Greenling* and *Gato* 3 800; 4 300 dived except *Jack* 4 470 dived, *Flasher, Greenling* and *Gato* 4 242 dived
**Length, feet (metres):** 278.5 *(84.9)* oa except *Jack* 297.4 *(90.7)* oa, *Flasher, Greenling* and *Gato* 292.2 *(89.1)*
**Beam, feet (metres):** 31.7 *(9.6)*
**Draught, efet (metres):** 28.4 *(8.7)*
**Missiles:** Fitted for 4 Harpoon (except in SSN 604-606, 612, 614 and 615)
**Torpedo tubes:** 4—21 in *(533 mm)* Mk 63 amidships
**A/S weapons:** SUBROC and A/S torpedoes
**Main machinery:** 1 pressurised-water cooled S5W (Westinghouse) reactor; 2 steam turbines, 15 000 shp; 1 shaft
**Speed, knots:** 20+ surfaced; 30+ dived
**Complement:** 143 (13 officers, 130 enlisted men)
**Commissioned:** 1962-68

They have a greater depth capability than previous SSNs and are the first to combine the SUBROC anti-submarine missile capability with the advanced BQQ 2 sonar system. The lead ship of the class, *Thresher* (SSN 593), was authorised in the FY 1957 new construction programme.

*Thresher* (SSN 593) was lost off the coast of New England on 10 April 1963 while on post-overhaul trials.

**Design:** *Jack* was built to a modified design to test a modified power plant.
*Flasher, Gato* and *Greenling* were modified during construction; fitted with SUBSAFE features, heavier machinery, and larger sail structures.
The sail structure height of the earlier submarines is 13 ft 9 in to 15 ft above the deck, with later submarines of this class having a sail height of 20 ft.

*Permit class ("Guardfish") 2/1986*
*(Dr. Giorgio Arra)*

| POTVIS | S 804 |
| TONIJN | S 805 |
| ZEEHOND | S 809 |

**Displacement, tons:** 1 140 standard; 1 520 surfaced; 1 830 dived ('Dolfijn' class): 1 509, 1 831 ('Potvis' class)

**Dimensions, feet (metres):** 260.9 × 25.8 × 15.7 *(79.5 × 7.8 × 4.8)* ('Dolfijn' class); 256.9 × 25.8 × 16.4 *(78.3 × 7.8 × 5)* ('Potvis' class)

**Torpedo tubes:** 8—21 in *(533 mm)* (4 bow, 4 stern)

**Main machinery:** 2 MAN diesels; 2 800 bhp ('Dolfijn' class); 2 Pielstick PA 4 diesels; 3 100 bhp ('Potvis' class) electric motors; 4 200 hp (4 400, 'Potvis'); 2 shafts

**Speed, knots:** 14.5 surfaced; 17 dived

**Complement:** 67

**Commissioned:** 1961-66

These submarines are of a triple-hull design, giving a diving depth 980 ft *(300 m)*. *Potvis* and *Tonijn*, originally voted for in 1949 with the other pair, but suspended for some years, had several modifications compared with *Dolfijn* and *Zeehond* and were officially considered to be a separate class; but modernisation of both classes has been completed, and all four boats were then almost identical. HSA M8 fire control. MAN diesels replaced by Pielstick in 'Potvis' class in 1977-79.

To be replaced by 'Walrus' class.

*Potvis/Dolfijn classes ("Tonijn")*
*9/1983 (*L & L van Ginderen*)*

| RESOLUTION | S 22 |
| REPULSE | S 23 |
| RENOWN | S 26 |
| REVENGE | S 27 |

**Displacement, tons:** 7 600 surfaced; 8 500 dived
**Dimensions, feet (metres):** 425 × 33 × 30 *(129.5 × 10.1 × 9.1)*
**Missiles:** SLBMs—16 Polaris A3
**Torpedo tubes:** 6—21 in *(533 mm)* (bow)
**Nuclear reactor:** 1 pressurised water-cooled (PWR 1)
**Main machinery:** Geared steam turbines; 1 shaft; 15 000 shp
**Speed, knots:** 20 surfaced; 25 dived
**Complement:** 143 (13 officers, 130 ratings); 2 crews
**Commissioned:** 1967-69

In February 1963 it was officially stated that it was intended to order four or five 7 000 ton nuclear powered submarines, each to carry 16 Polaris missiles, and it was planned that the first would be on patrol in 1968. Their hulls and machinery would be of British design. As well as building two submarines Vickers (Shipbuilding) would give lead yard service to the builder of the other two. Four Polaris submarines were in fact ordered in May 1963. The plan to build a fifth Polaris submarine was cancelled on 15 February 1965. Britain's first SSBN, *Resolution,* put to sea on 22 June 1967 and completed six weeks trial in the Firth of Clyde and Atlantic on 17 August 1967.

*Resolution class ("Resolution")*
*8/1982 (*Royal Navy*)*

| | |
|---|---|
| **NAZARIO SAURO** | S 518 |
| **FECIA DI COSSATO** | S 519 |
| **LEONARDO DA VINCI** | S 520 |
| **GUGLIELMO MARCONI** | S 521 |

**Displacement, tons:** 1 456 surfaced; 1 631 dived
**Dimensions, feet (metres):** 210 × 22.5 × 18.9 *(63.9 × 6.8 × 5.7)*
**Torpedo tubes:** 6—21 in *(533 mm)* (bow) (6 reloads) (all Type 184)
**Main machinery:** 3 GMT A210 16NM diesel generators; 3 650 bhp; 1 electric motor; 3 210 hp; 1 shaft
**Speed, knots:** 11 surfaced; 19 dived; 12 (snorting)
**Range, miles:** 3 000 at 11 knots surfaced; 2 500 snorting at 12 knots; 250 dived at 4 knots; 19 dived at 19 knots
**Endurance:** 45 days
**Complement:** 45 (including 4 for training)
**Commissioned:** 1980-82

Two of this class were originally ordered in 1967 but were cancelled in the following year. Reinstated in the building programme in 1972. Second pair provided for in Legge Navale and ordered 12 February 1976.

*Sauro class ("Leonardo da Vinci")*
*6/1981 (*Dr. Giorgio Arra*)*

| | |
|---|---|
| **SKATE** | SSN 578 |
| **SWORDFISH** | SSN 579 |
| **SARGO** | SSN 583 |

**Displacement, tons:** 2 310 light; 2 360 full load
(578-9); 2 384 light; 2 547 full load (583)
**Dimensions, feet (metres):** 267.7 × 25 × 22 *(81.5
× 7.6 × 6.7)*
**Torpedo tubes:** 8—21 in *(533 mm)* 6 bow; 2
stern (short)
**Main machinery:** 1 pressurised-water cooled
S3W (Westinghouse) reactor in *Skate* and
*Sargo*, 1 pressurised-water cooled S4W
(Westinghouse) in *Swordfish*; 2 steam turbines
(Westinghouse); 6 600 shp; 2 shafts
**Speed, knots:** 20+ surfaced; 25+ dived
**Complement:** 139
**Commissioned:** 1957-58

The first production model nuclear-powered
submarines, similar in design to the first of this
type, *Nautilus* but smaller. *Skate* and *Swordfish*
were authorised in the FY 1955 new construction
programme and *Sargo* in FY 1956.

*Skate* was the first submarine to make a
completely submerged Transatlantic crossing. In
1958 she established a (then) record of 31 days
submerged with a sealed atmosphere, on 11
August 1958 she passed under the ice at the
North Pole during a polar cruise, and on 17
March 1959 she became the first submarine to
surface at the North Pole.

*Skate class ("Seadragon" now
deleted) 3/1978 (*Dr. Giorgio Arra*)*

| | |
|---|---|
| **SKIPJACK** | SSN 585 |
| **SCAMP** | SSN 588 |
| **SCULPIN** | SSN 590 |
| **SHARK** | SSN 591 |
| **SNOOK** | SSN 592 |

**Displacement, tons:** 3 075 surfaced; 3 513 dived
**Dimensions, feet (metres):** 251.7 × 31.5 × 29.4
  *(76.7 × 9.6 × 8.9)*
**Torpedo tubes:** 6—21 in *(533 mm)* bow (Mk 59)
**A/S weapons:** A/S torpedoes
**Main machinery:** 1 pressurised-water cooled
  S5W (Westinghouse) reactor; 2 steam turbines
  (Westinghouse in *Skipjack;* General Electric in
  others); 15 000 shp; 1 shaft
**Speed, knots:** 16+ surfaced; 30+ dived
**Complement:** 141-143
**Commissioned:** 1958-61

Combine the high-speed endurance of nuclear
propulsion with the high-speed 'tear-drop'
'Albacore' hull design. *Skipjack* was authorised
in the FY 1956 new construction programme and
the five other submarines of this class were
authorised in FY 1957. These submarines are still
considered suitable for 'first line' service.

**Design:** *Skipjack* was the first US nuclear
submarine built to the 'tear-drop' design. These
submarines have a single propeller shaft (instead
of two in earlier nuclear submarines) and their
diving planes are mounted on sail structures to
improve underwater manoeuvrability. No after
torpedo tubes are fitted because of their tapering
sterns.

*Skipjack class ("Scamp") 12/1982*
*(G. Gyssels)*

| RUBIS | S 601 |
| SAPHIR | S 602 |
| CASABIANCA | S 603 |
| PERLE | S 604 |

**Displacement, tons:** 2 385 surfaced; 2 670 dived
**Dimensions, feet (metres):** 236.5 × 24.9 × 21
  *(72.1 × 7.6 × 6.4)*
**Torpedo tubes:** 4—21 in *(533 mm)* (18 torpedoes
  or mines)
**Missiles:** Tube-launched SM 39 (see note)
**Main machinery:** 1 nuclear reactor; 48 MW; 2
  turbo alternators; 1 main motor; 1 shaft with
  emergency electric motor
**Speed, knots:** 25
**Complement:** 66 (9 officers, 35 petty officers, 22
  junior ratings)
**Commissioned:** 1983-87 (2 more on order)

A new class of fleet submarines with the first
included in the 1974 programme. The armament,
sonar and fire control equipment are improved
versions of those in the 'Agosta' class. This class
is being followed by a modified design, three of
which are planned to commission in 1992-94.
The first of these, S 606, was ordered on 17
October 1984; S 607 approved under FY 1986
programme.

**Missiles:** The SM 39, an adaptation of the MM 38
Exocet, will have a range of about 50 km.
Embarked from January 1985 in S 602 and
following submarines.

**Preliminary cruise:** *Rubis* (after preliminary trials
beginning June 1980), carried out preliminary
cruise early 1982 with second part completed in
November 1982. *Saphir* began preliminary trials
26 June 1982.

*SNA 72 type ("Rubis") 1983*
*(Dr. Giorgio Arra)*

| | |
|---|---|
| **STURGEON** | SSN 637 |
| **WHALE** | SSN 638 |
| **TAUTOG** | SSN 639 |
| **GRAYLING** | SSN 646 |
| **POGY** | SSN 647 |
| **ASPRO** | SSN 648 |
| **SUNFISH** | SSN 649 |
| **PARGO** | SSN 650 |
| **QUEENFISH** | SSN 651 |
| **PUFFER** | SSN 652 |
| **RAY** | SSN 653 |
| **SAND LANCE** | SSN 660 |
| **LAPON** | SSN 661 |
| **GURNARD** | SSN 662 |
| **HAMMERHEAD** | SSN 663 |
| **SEA DEVIL** | SSN 664 |
| **GUITARRO** | SSN 665 |
| **HAWKBILL** | SSN 666 |
| **BERGALL** | SSN 667 |
| **SPADEFISH** | SSN 668 |
| **SEAHORSE** | SSN 669 |
| **FINBACK** | SSN 670 |
| **PINTADO** | SSN 672 |
| **FLYING FISH** | SSN 673 |
| **TREPANG** | SSN 674 |
| **BLUEFISH** | SSN 675 |
| **BILLFISH** | SSN 676 |
| **DRUM** | SSN 677 |
| **ARCHERFISH** | SSN 678 |
| **SILVERSIDES** | SSN 679 |
| **WILLIAM H. BATES** (ex-*Redfish*) | SSN 680 |
| **BATFISH** | SSN 681 |
| **TUNNY** | SSN 682 |
| **PARCHE** | SSN 683 |
| **CAVALLA** | SSN 684 |
| **L. MENDEL RIVERS** | SSN 686 |
| **RICHARD B. RUSSELL** | SSN 687 |

*Sturgeon class ("Pogy") 6/1983*
*(Dr. Giorgio Arra)*

**Displacement, tons:** 3 640 standard; 4 640 dived
**Dimensions, feet (metres):** 292.2 × 31.7 × 26 *(89 × 9.5 × 7.9)* (see *Design* note)
**Missiles:** Fitted or being fitted for 4 Harpoon and 8 Tomahawk
**Torpedo tubes:** 4—21 in *(533 mm)* Mk 63 amidships
**A/S weapons:** SUBROC and A/S torpedoes
**Main machinery:** 1 pressurised-water cooled S5W (Westinghouse) reactor; 2 steam turbines; 15 000 shp; 1 shaft
**Speed, knots:** 20+ surfaced; 30+ dived
**Complement:** 141 (13 officers, 128 enlisted men)
**Commissioned:** 1967-75

The 37 'Sturgeon' class attack submarines were the largest US Navy group of nuclear-powered ships built to the same design until the advent of the 'Los Angeles' class.

**Conversion:** Under FY 1982 programme *Cavalla* was converted at Pearl Harbor in August-December 1982 to have a secondary role as 'Troop Transport'. This includes a Swimmer Delivery Vehicle stowage.

**Design:** These submarines are slightly larger than the 'Thresher' class and can be identified by their taller sail structure and the lower position of their diving planes on the sail.

**Submersibles:** *Hawkbill* and *Pintado* have been modified to carry and support the Navy's Deep Submergence Rescue Vehicles (DSRV).

| | |
|---|---|
| SWIFTSURE | S 126 |
| SOVEREIGN | S 108 |
| SUPERB | S 109 |
| SCEPTRE | S 104 |
| SPARTAN | S 105 |
| SPLENDID | S 106 |

**Displacement, tons:** 4 000 light; 4 400 standard; 4 900 dived

**Dimensions, feet (metres):** 272 × 32.3 × 27 *(82.9 × 9.8 × 8.2)*

**Torpedo tubes:** 5—21 in *(533 mm)* (20 reloads)

**Nuclear reactor:** 1 pressurised water-cooled

**Main machinery:** 2 General Electric geared steam turbines; 15 000 shp; 2 Paxman auxiliary diesels; 4 000 hp; 1 shaft; W H Allen turbo-generator sets

**Speed, knots:** 30+ dived

**Complement:** 116

**Commissioned:** 1973-81

Compared with the 'Valiant' class submarines these are slightly shorter with a fuller form, with the fore-planes set further forward, with one less torpedo tube and with a deeper diving depth and faster.

**Armament:** Refitted to carry Sub Harpoon.

*Swiftsure class ("Superb") 1976*
*(Royal Navy)*

## ITALY

**LIVIO PIOMARTA**
  (ex-USS *Trigger*)                                    S 515
**ROMEO ROMEI**
  (ex-USS *Harder*)                                     S 516

## TURKEY

**HIZIRREIS** (ex-USS *Gudgeon*)                        S 342
**PIRIREIS** (ex-USS *Tang*)                            S 343

**Displacement, tons:** 2 050 surfaced; 2 700 dived
**Dimensions, feet (metres):** 287 × 27.3 × 19 *(87.4 × 8.3 × 5.8)*
**Torpedo tubes:** 8—21 in *(533 mm)* (6 bow, 2 stern)
**Main machinery:** 3 diesels; 4 500 shp; 2 shafts; 2 electric motors; 5 600 hp
**Speed, knots:** 15.5 surfaced; 16 dived
**Range, miles:** 11 000 at 11 knots
**Complement:** 75 (7 officers, 68 men)
**Commissioned:** 1952

## ITALY

Transferred as follows: *Romeo Romei* 20 February 1974, *Livio Piomarta* 10 July 1973. Subsequently refitted at Philadelphia Navy Yard. Despite their age these two boats will continue in service, with main emphasis on training.

## TURKEY

**Commissioned:** 1951-52
S 343 transferred January 1980—commissioned 21 March 1980. S 342 transferred by lease 30 September 1983. On loan for five years.

*Tang class ("Pirireis") 3/1980 (*Selçuk Emre*)*

**ATTILIO BAGNOLINI**          S 505
**ENRICO TOTI**                S 506
**ENRICO DANDOLO**             S 513
**LAZZARO MOCENIGO**           S 514

**Displacement, tons:** 460 standard; 524
    surfaced; 582 dived
**Dimensions, feet (metres):** 151.5 × 15.4 × 13.1
    *(46.2 × 4.7 × 4)*
**Torpedo tubes:** 4—21 in *(533 mm)*
**Main machinery:** 2 Fiat MB 820 N/I diesels, 1
    electric motor, diesel-electric drive; 2 200 hp; 1
    shaft
**Speed, knots:** 14 surfaced; 15 dived
**Range, miles:** 3 000 at 5 knots (surfaced)
**Complement:** 26 (4 officers, 22 men)
**Commissioned:** 1968-69

Italy's first indigenously-built submarines since
the Second World War.

*Toti class ("Enrico Toti")*

| | |
|---|---|
| TRAFALGAR | S 107 |
| TURBULENT | S 87 |
| TIRELESS | S 88 |
| TORBAY | S 90 |
| TRENCHANT | S 91 |
| TALENT | S 92 |
| TRIUMPH | S 93 |

**Displacement, tonnes:** 4 200 light; 5 208 dived
**Dimensions, feet (metres):** 280.1 × 32.1 × 26.9 *(85.4 × 9.8 × 8.2)*
**Torpedo tubes:** 5—21 in *(533 mm)* (20 reloads)
**Nuclear reactor:** 1 pressurised water cooled (PWR 1)
**Main machinery:** 2 General Electric geared steam turbines; 15 000 shp; 2 Paxman auxiliary diesels; 4 000 hp; 1 shaft; W H Allen turbo-generator sets
**Speed, knots:** 32 dived
**Complement:** 130
**Commissioned:** 1983-90

The first of an improved class of Fleet Submarines was ordered in September 1977. *Turbulent* ordered 28 July 1978 with *Tireless* ordered 5 July 1979, *Torbay* on 26 June 1981, *Trenchant* on 22 March 1983 and *Talent* on 10 September 1984, *Triumph* on 3 January 1986.
**Armament:** carry Sub-Harpoons plus torpedoes or mines.

*Trafalgar class ("Tireless") 10/1985*

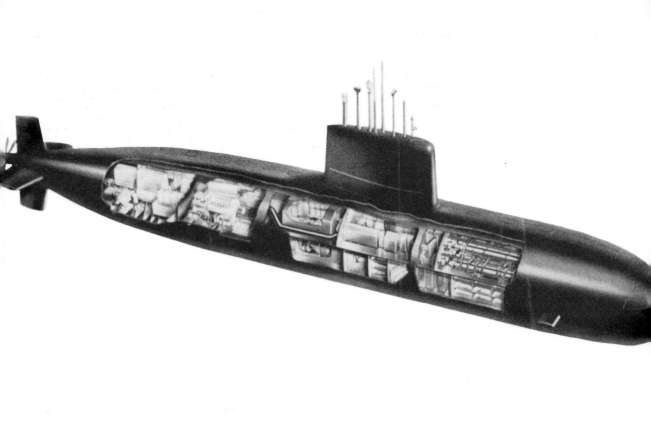

UPHOLDER                    S 40
UNSEEN
URSULA
UNICORN

**Displacement, tonnes:** 2 400 dived
**Dimensions, feet (metres):** 230.6 × 25 × 17.7
   *(70.3 × 7.6 × 5.5)*
**Torpedo tubes:** 6—21 in *(533 mm)* (12 reloads)
**Main machinery:** 2 Paxman Valenta 1 600 RPA-
   200 S diesels; 2 GEC alternators; 1 GEC
   electric motor; 5 400 hp
**Speed, knots:** 12 surfaced; 20 dived
**Range, miles:** 8 000 at 8 knots (surfaced)
**Complement:** 44 (7 officers, 13 senior ratings,
   24 junior ratings)
**Commissioned:** First due 1986

The need for the provision of a new class of non-
nuclear submarines was acknowledged in the
late 1970s and in 1979 the Type 2400 design
was first revealed. This was larger than first
requested. The above data is somewhat tentative.
First boat ordered from Vickers SEL 2 November
1983—possible completion 1987. Further three
ordered from Vickers on 3 January 1986. No
decision on timing and total numbers has yet
been reached, although a total of ten seems
realistic.

*'Upholder' class*

| | |
|---|---|
| VALIANT | S 102 |
| WARSPITE | S 103 |
| CHURCHILL | S 46 |
| CONQUEROR | S 48 |
| COURAGEOUS | S 50 |

**Displacement, tons:** 4 000 light; 4 300 standard; 4 800 dived
**Dimensions, feet (metres):** 285 × 33.2 × 27 *(86.9 × 10.1 × 8.2)*
**Torpedo tubes:** 6—21 in *(533 mm)* (26 reloads)
**Nuclear reactor:** 1 pressurised water-cooled
**Main machinery:** English Electric geared steam turbines; 1 shaft; 15 000 shp
**Speed, knots:** 28 dived
**Complement**: 116
**Commissioned:** 1966-71

It was announced on 31 August 1960 that the contract for a second nuclear powered submarine *(Valiant)* to follow *Dreadnought* had been awarded to Vickers Ltd, the principal sub-contractors being Vickers-Armstrong (Engineers) Ltd, for the machinery and its installation, and Rolls-Royce and Associates for the nuclear steam raising plant. She was originally scheduled to be completed in September 1965, but work was held up by the Polaris programme.

*Valiant/Churchill classes ("Valiant")*
*6/1977 (*C. & S. Taylor*)*

| | |
|---|---|
| **WALRUS** | S 802 |
| **ZEELEEUW** | S 803 |
| **DOLFYN** | |
| **BRUINVIS** | |

**Displacement, tons:** 1 900 standard; 2 450 surfaced; 2 800 dived

**Dimensions, feet (metres):** 223.1 × 27.6 × 21.6 *(67.7 × 8.4 × 6.6)*

**Torpedo tubes:** 4—21 in *(533 mm)*

**Main machinery:** Diesel-electric; 3 SEMT-Pielstick 12 PA4-V200 diesels; 6 910 hp; 1 Holec electric motor; 1 shaft (7- bladed propeller)

**Speed, knots:** 13 surfaced; 20 dived

**Complement:** 49

**Commissioned:** due 1988-93

In the 1975 Navy Estimates money was set aside for design work on this class and a contract for the building of the first was signed 16 June 1979, the second was on 17 December 1979.

These will be an improvement on the 'Zwaardvis' class with similar dimensions and identical silhouette.

In 1981 various changes to the design were made which will result in a delay of 1-2 years.

*Walrus* trials to start in April 1987 and *Zeeleeuw* in February 1988.

*Dolfyn* and *Bruinvis* ordered 16 August 1985. Prefabrication started late 1985.

**Future:** Construction of another submarine is planned to start in 1990s on completion of *Dolfyn* and *Bruinvis*.

*Walrus, 1980 (*Royal Netherlands Navy*)*

| | |
|---|---|
| **ZWAARDVIS** | S 806 |
| **TIJGERHAAI** | S 807 |

**Displacement, tons:** 2 350 surfaced; 2 640 dived
**Dimensions, feet (metres):** 216.5 × 27.6 × 23.3
  *(66 × 8.4 × 7.1)*
**Torpedo tubes:** 6—21 in *(533 mm)* (bow)
**Main machinery:** Diesel-electric; 3 diesel
  generators; 1 shaft; 4 200 shp
**Speed, knots:** 13 surfaced; 20 dived
**Complement:** 67
**Commissioned:** 1972

In the 1964 Navy Estimates a first instalment was
approved for the construction of two
conventionally powered submarines of tear-drop
design. HSA M8 fire control.

**Mid-life conversion:** To be carried out in 1988
*(Tijgerhaai)* and 1989-90 *(Zwaardvis)*. New
Eledone sonar and Signaal fire control to be fitted
plus certain minor improvements.

*Zwaardvis class ("Zwaardvis")*
*10/1977 (*Michael D. J. Lennon*)*

| U 1 | S 180 |
| U 2 | S 181 |
| U 9 | S 188 |
| U 10 | S 189 |
| U 11 | S 190 |
| U 12 | S 191 |

**Displacement, tons:** 419 surfaced; 450 dived
**Dimensions, feet (metres):** 144 × 15.1 × 14.1
  *(43.9 × 4.6 × 4.3)*
**Torpedo tubes:** 8—21 in *(533 mm)* (bow) (no
  reloads)
**Main machinery:** 2 Maybach (MTU) diesels; total
  1 200 bhp; 1 Siemens electric motor; 1 500
  bhp; single screw
**Speed, knots:** 10 surfaced; 17 dived
**Complement:** 22 (4 officers, 18 men)
**Commissioned:** 1967-69

All built in floating docks. First submarines designed and built by the Federal Republic of Germany since the end of the Second World War. The original U 1 and U 2 which were commissioned in March and May 1962 were not satisfactory and were scrapped. U 9-12 have hulls of different steel alloys of non-magnetic properties. U 3 of this class lent to Norway on 10 July 1962 and temporarily named *Kobben* (S 310), was returned to West Germany in 1964 and decommissioned on 15 September 1967 for disposal. No plans for modernisation but some are being modified for trials of new equipment. The class will have to serve until replaced by Type 211 in the 1990s.

*Type 205 ("U 11") 6/1984 (*L & L
van Ginderen*)*

| U 13 | S 192 |
|------|-------|
| U 14 | S 193 |
| U 15 | S 194 |
| U 16 | S 195 |
| U 17 | S 196 |
| U 18 | S 197 |
| U 19 | S 198 |
| U 20 | S 199 |
| U 21 | S 170 |
| U 22 | S 171 |
| U 23 | S 172 |
| U 24 | S 173 |
| U 25 | S 174 |
| U 26 | S 175 |
| U 27 | S 176 |
| U 28 | S 177 |
| U 29 | S 178 |
| U 30 | S 179 |

**Displacement, tons:** 450 surfaced; 498 dived
**Dimensions, feet (metres):** 159.4 × 15.1 × 14.8 *(48.6 × 4.6 × 4.5)*
**Torpedo tubes:** 8—21 in *(533 mm)* (bow) (no reloads)
**Main machinery:** MTU diesel-electric; diesels; 1 500 hp; 1 main motor; 1 800 hp; 1 shaft
**Speed, knots:** 10 surfaced; 17 dived
**Range, miles:** 4 500 at 5 knots (surfaced)
**Complement:** 22 (4 officers, 18 men)
**Commissioned:** 1973-75

Authorised on 7 June 1969 from Howaldtswerke Deutsche Werft (8) and Rheinstahl Nordseewerke, Emden (10).

**Modernisation:** Howaldtswerke, Kiel is the main contractor for the modernisation of 12 boats of this class from 1988-91 to extend service life into 21st century.

*Type 206 ("U 20") 6 / 1984 (*L & L van Ginderen*)*

| | |
|---|---|
| **ULA** | S 300 |
| **UTSIRA** | S 301 |
| **UTSTEIN** | S 302 |
| **UTVAER** | S 303 |
| **UTHAUG** | S 304 |
| **SKLINNA** | S 305 |
| **SKOLPEN** | S 306 |
| **STADT** | S 307 |
| **STORD** | S 308 |
| **SVENNER** | S 309 |
| **KAURA** | S 315 |
| **KYA** | S 317 |
| **KOBBEN** | S 318 |
| **KUNNA** | S 319 |

**Displacement, tons:** 370 standard; 435 dived
**Dimensions, feet (metres):** 148.9 × 15 × 14 *(45.4 × 4.6 × 4.3)*
**Torpedo tubes:** 8—21 in *(533 mm)* (bow) (8 torpedoes carried)
**Main machinery:** 2 MB 820 Maybach-Mercedes-Benz (MTU) diesels; 1 200 bhp; electric drive; 1 500 hp; 1 shaft
**Speed, knots:** 12 surfaced; 18 dived
**Complement:** 18 (5 officers, 13 men) (17, *Svenner*)
**Commissioned:** 1965-67

It was announced in July 1959 that the USA and Norway would share equally the cost of these submarines. These are a development of IKL Type 205 (West German U4-U8) with increased diving depth.

**Modernisation:** Six are to be modernised with high priority.

**Note:** Denmark is purchasing three submarines of the '207' class from Norway to replace 'Delfinen' class. Final government approval with funds granted December 1985.

*Type 207 ("Skolpen") (*Royal Norwegian Navy*)*

## GREECE

| | |
|---|---|
| **GLAVKOS*** | S 110 |
| **NEREUS*** | S 111 |
| **TRITON*** | S 112 |
| **PROTEUS*** | S 113 |
| **POSYDON** | S 116 |
| **AMPHITRITE** | S 117 |
| **OKEANOS** | S 118 |
| **PONTOS** | S 119 |

* Type 1100

## TURKEY (TYPE 1200)

| | |
|---|---|
| **ATILAY** | S 347 |
| **SALDIRAY** | S 348 |
| **BATIRAY** | S 349 |
| **YILDIRAY** | S 350 |
| **DOGANAY** | S 351 |
| **TITIRAY** | S 352 |

*Type 209 ("Atilay") 2/1975 (Reiner Nerlich)*

**Displacement, tons:** 1 100 surfaced; 1 210 dived (1 285, second four)
**Dimensions, feet (metres):** 178.4 × 20.3 × 17.9 *(54.4 × 6.2 × 5.5)* (second four 183.4 ft *(55.9 m)*)
**Torpedo tubes:** 8—21 in *(533 mm)* (with reloads) bow
**Main machinery:** Diesel-electric; 4 MTU diesels; 4 Siemens generators; 7 040 kW; 1 Siemens electric motor; 3 700 kW; 1 shaft
**Speed, knots:** 11 surfaced; 21.5 dived
**Endurance:** 50 days
**Complement:** 31 (6 officers, 25 ratings)
**Commissioned:** 1971-72 (type 1100); 1979-80 (type 1200)

Designed by Ingenieurkontor, Lübeck for construction by Howaldtswerke, Kiel and sale by Ferrostaal, Essen all acting as a consortium.

## GREECE

Second four ordered 1975-76.

## TURKEY

**Commissioned:** 1975-86

**Future construction:** This class of submarines is the first ever built in Turkey. Up to a total of 12 is planned, probably building at one a year to replace ex-US Navy boats. Assistance being given at Gölcük by Howaldtswerke.

**CLEMENCEAU** R 98
**FOCH** R 99

**Displacement, tons:** 27 307 standard; 32 780 full load
**Dimensions, feet (metres):** 869.4 × 104.1 hull (with bulges) × 28.2 *(265 × 31.7 × 8.6)*
**Width, feet (metres):** 168 *(51.2)* oa (flight deck and sponsons)
**Aircraft:** Capacity 40 (4 Flights) 2 of Super Etendard, 1 of Crusaders, 1 of Breguet Alizé (see *Aircraft* note)
**Catapults:** 2 Mitchell-Brown steam, Mk BS 5
**Missiles:** See *Modernisation* note
**Guns:** 8—3.9 in *(100 mm)* automatic in single turrets (see *Modernisation* note)
**Armour:** Flight deck, island superstructure and bridges, hull (over machinery spaces and magazines)
**Main engines:** 2 sets Parsons geared turbines; 2 shafts; 126 000 shp
**Boilers:** 6; steam pressure 640 psi *(45 kg/cm$^2$)*, superheat 842°F *(450°C)*
**Speed, knots:** 32
**Oil fuel, tons:** 3 720
**Range, miles:** 7 500 at 18 knots; 4 800 at 24 knots; 3 500 at full power
**Complement:** 1 338 (64 officers, 1 274 men)
**Commissioned:** 1961-63

First aircraft carriers designed as such and built from the keel to be completed in France. Authorised in 1953 and 1955 respectively. *Clemenceau* ordered from Brest Dockyard on 28 May 1954 and begun in November 1955. *Foch* begun at Chantiers de l'Atlantique at St. Nazaire, Penhoet-Loire, in a special dry dock (contract provided for the construction of the hull and propelling machinery) and completed by Brest Dockyard.

*Clemenceau* refitted in 1978 to accommodate Super Etendard aircraft and tactical nuclear weapons. *Foch* had a similar refit to *Clemenceau*'s from July 1980 to 15 August 1981. She returned to service at the end of November and will have a further refit 1987-88.

Under current plans *Clemenceau* is due to pay off in 1995 and *Foch* in 1998.

**Aircraft:** Each flight has about ten aircraft. In addition two Super Frelon and two Alouette III helicopters are carried. Etendard IV P may also be carried for reconnaissance.

**Modernisation:** *Clemenceau* started a twelve month refit 1 September 1985. This includes the replacement of four 100 mm guns by two Crotale, retubing of boilers and other major engine overhauls, fitting of stronger aircraft lifts and catapults, modernisation of communications and electronics, fitting of Dagaie, new long range air warning radar and passive radar detection system, and modernised action information organisation. Presumably *Foch* will have a similar modernisation in her 1987-88 refit.

*Clemenceau class ("Clemenceau")*
*6/1983 (G. Gyssels)*

**DÉDALO** (ex-USS *Cabot* AVT 3,
   ex-*CVL 28*, ex-*Wilmington* CL 79)      R 01

**Displacement, tons:** 13 000 standard; 16 416
   full load
**Dimensions, feet (metres):** 623 × 71.5 (hull) × 26
   *(189.9 × 21.8 × 7.9)*
**Width, feet (metres):** 109 *(33.2)*
**Aircraft:** 7 Harriers (5 AV-8A, 2 TAV-8A)
   (Matador) 20 helicopters (ASW/Sea Kings—
   Combat/Huey Cobras—Landings/specially
   embarked Bell 212s)
**Guns:** 22—40 mm/L60 (1 quad, 9 twin Mk 2 and
   Mk 1)
**Armour:** 2 to 5 in sides; 2 to 3 in deck
**Main engines:** GE geared turbines; 4 shafts;
   100 000 shp
**Boilers:** 4 Babcock & Wilcox
**Speed, knots:** 24
**Range, miles:** 7 200 at 15 knots
**Oil fuel, tons:** 1 800
**Complement:** 1 112 (without Air Groups)
**Commissioned:** 1943

Completed as an aircraft carrier from the hull of a
'Cleveland' class cruiser. Originally carried over
40 aircraft. Converted with strengthened flight
and hangar decks, large port side catapult,
revised magazine arrangements, new electronic
gear, with stability corrected to offset the added
top-weight. Hangar capacity altered to take 20
aircraft. Flight deck: 545 × 108 ft *(166.1 × 32.9 m)*.

Reactivated and modernised at Philadelphia
Naval Shipyard, where she was transferred to
Spain on 30 August 1967, on loan for five years.
Purchased 5 December 1973. Fleet flagship. Due
to pay off on completion of *Principe de Asturias*.

**Aircraft:** Hangar capacity—18 Sea Kings. Six
more can be spotted on flight deck. Typical
embarked strength, four groups of aircraft at least
one with Harriers, one with Sea Kings, one with
EWF AB 212s and one as required for operations.
Five to seven aircraft groups of four machines
can be handled aboard.

*Dedalo (ex-US "Independence"
class) 9/1981 (*Commander Aldo
Fraccaroli*)*

**ENTERPRISE** CVN 65

**Displacement, tons:** 73 502 light; 75 700 standard; 90 970 full load
**Dimensions, feet (metres):** 1 088 × 133 × 39 *(331.6 × 40.5 × 11.9)*
**Flight deck width, feet (metres):** 252 *(76.8)* max
**Aircraft:** Approx 90
**Catapults:** 4 steam (C13)
**Missiles:** 3 NATO Sea Sparrow launchers (Mk 57)
**Guns:** 3 Phalanx Mk 15 CIWS systems; 2—40 mm Mk II saluting guns; 3—20 mm Mk 68
**Main engines:** 4 geared steam turbines (Westinghouse); 4 shafts; 280 000 shp
**Nuclear reactors:** 8 pressurised-water cooled A2W (Westinghouse)
**Speed, knots:** Approx 35
**Complement:** 3 353 (163 officers, approx 3 190 enlisted men) plus 2 480 assigned to attack air wing for a total of 5 833
**Commissioned:** 1961

At the time of her construction, *Enterprise* was the largest warship ever built and is rivalled in size only by the nuclear-powered 'Nimitz' class ships. *Enterprise* was authorised in the FY 1958 new construction programme. She was launched only 31 months after her keel was laid down. The cost of *Enterprise* was $451.3 million. As a result of this high cost five planned ships were cancelled.

Underwent a refit/overhaul at Puget Sound

Naval SY, Bremerton, Washington from January 1979 to March 1982. Cost $276.7 million.

**Design:** Built to a modified 'Forrestal' class design. Nuclear propulsion eliminated requirement for smoke stack and boiler air intakes.

A re-shaping of the island took place in her 1979-82 refit. This included the removal of the mast and dome (which carried obsolete ECM gear) which were replaced with a mast similar to that of the 'Nimitz' class.

*Enterprise* has four deck-edge lifts—two forward of the island and one on each side abaft the island.

**Engineering:** *Enterprise* was the world's second nuclear-powered warship (the cruiser *Long Beach* was completed a few months earlier).

The first of the eight reactors installed in *Enterprise* achieved initial criticality on 2 December 1960, shortly after the carrier was launched. After three years of operation during which she steamed more than 207 000 miles, *Enterprise* was overhauled and refuelled from November 1964 to July 1965. Her second set of cores provided about 300 000 miles steaming. The eight cores initially installed in *Enterprise* cost $64 million; the second set cost about $20 million.

There are two reactors for each of the ship's four shafts. The eight reactors feed 32 heat exchangers.

*Enterprise class ("Enterprise")*
*8/1985 (Dr. Giorgio Arra)*

**HORNET** CVS 12
**BENNINGTON** CVS 20

**Displacement, tons:** 33 000 standard; 40 600 full load
**Dimensions, feet (metres):** 899 × 101 × 31 *(274 × 30.7 × 9.4)*
**Flight deck width, feet (metres):** 172 *(52.4)*
**Catapults:** 2 hydraulic (H-8)
**Aircraft:** 45 (including 16 to 18 helicopters)
**Guns:** 4—5 in *(127 mm)*/38 (single Mk 24)
**Main engines:** 4 geared turbines (Westinghouse); 4 shafts; 150 000 shp
**Boilers:** 8 Babcock & Wilcox
**Speed, knots:** 30+
**Complement:** 1 615 (115 officers, approx 1 500 enlisted men) plus approx 800 assigned to ASW air group for a total of 2 400 per ship
**Commissioned:** 1943-44

Survivors of the 24 'Essex' class fleet carriers laid down during the Second World War. Both ships were extensively modernised during the 1950s; however, they lack the steam catapults and other features of the 'Hancock' and 'Intrepid' classes.

**Modernisation:** These ships have been modernised under several programmes to increase their ability to operate advanced aircraft and to improve sea keeping. Also modernised to improve anti-submarine capabilities under the Fleet Rehabilitation and Modernisation (FRAM II) programme.

*Bennington*, 1961. *(L. and L. van Ginderen)*

| | |
|---|---|
| **FORRESTAL** | CV 59 |
| **SARATOGA** | CV 60 |
| **RANGER** | CV 61 |
| **INDEPENDENCE** | CV 62 |

**Displacement, tons:** 59 060 (CV 59, 60), 60 000 (CV 61, 62) standard; 79 250 (CV 59), 80 383 (60), 81 163 (61), 80 643 (62) full load
**Length, feet (metres):** *Forrestal:* 1 086 *(331), Saratoga:* 1 063 *(324), Ranger:* 1 071 *(326.4), Independence:* 1 070 *(326.1)*
**Beam, feet (metres):** 129.5 *(39.5)*
**Draught, feet (metres):** 37 *(11.3)*
**Flight deck width, feet (metres):** 252 *(76.8)* max
**Catapults:** 4 steam (2—C7 and 2—C11 in 59 and 60; 4—C7 others)
**Aircraft:** Approx 90
**Missiles:** 3 Basic Point Defence Missile Systems (BPDMS) launchers with Sea Sparrow missiles
**Guns:** 3—20 mm Mk 16 Phalanx CIWS (except CV 61); 4—40 mm saluting guns
**Main engines:** 4 geared turbines (Westinghouse); 4 shafts; 260 000 shp *(Forrestal);* 280 000 shp (remainder)
**Boilers:** 8 Babcock & Wilcox
**Speed, knots:** *Forrestal:* 33; others: 34
**Oil fuel, tons:** 7 800
**Complement:** 3 019 (160 officers, 2 859 enlisted men) plus 2 480 air wing; Total: 5 499
**Commissioned:** 1955-59

*Forrestal* was the world's first aircraft carrier built after the Second World War. The *Forrestal* design drew heavily from the aircraft carrier *United States* (CVA 58) which was cancelled immediately after being laid down in April 1949.

**Appearance:** Funnel height of *Forrestal* and *Independence* increased by 10 ft in 1980.

**Design:** The 'Forrestal' class ships were the first aircraft carriers designed and built specifically to operate jet- propelled aircraft. *Forrestal* was redesigned early in construction to incorporate British-developed angled flight deck and steam catapults. These were the first US aircraft carriers built with an enclosed bow area to improve seaworthiness. Other features include armoured flight deck and advanced underwater protection and internal compartmentation to reduce effects of conventional and nuclear attack. Mast configurations differ.

*Forrestal class ("Ranger") 1/1986
(Dr. Giorgio Arra)*

**GIUSEPPE GARIBALDI**                C 551

**Displacement, tons:** 10 000 standard; 13 500 full load

**Dimensions, feet (metres):** 591.1 × 76.8 × 22 *(180.2 × 23.4 × 6.7)*

**Flight deck, feet (metres):** 570.7 × 99.7 *(174 × 30.4)*

**Aircraft:** 16 Sea King helicopters (12 in hangar, 4 on deck) or equivalent

**Missiles:** SSM; 4 Teseo 2 launchers for Otomat Mk 2; SAM; 2 Albatros systems with octuple launchers for Aspide missiles (48 missiles)

**Guns:** 6—40 mm/70 L Breda MB guns (twin) with Dardo control system

**A/S weapons:** 6 Mk 32 A/S torpedo tubes (2 triple) for Mk 46 or Whitehead Motofides A 244 torpedoes; helicopter torpedoes

**Main engines:** COGAG; 4 Fiat/GE LM2500 gas turbines; 2 shafts (5-bladed propellers); 80 000 hp (100 000 max)

**Speed, knots:** 30

**Range, miles:** 7 000 at 20 knots (cruising)

**Complement:** 550 (ship), 230 (air group) (accommodation 825 including Flag and staff)

**Commissioned:** 1985

Contract awarded 21 November 1977.

The design was changed considerably. To replace *Andrea Doria* and *Caio Duilio*. Design work completed February 1980 and engineering work began in March 1980. Started sea trials 3 December 1984. Flagship of the fleet, replacing *Vittorio Veneto*.

**Aircraft:** Fitted with 6° Ski-jump and VSTOL operating equipment. So far, however, the Air Force has consistently vetoed the Navy's acquisition of these aircraft. The MoD has introduced a Bill to allow the navy to operate their own fleet air arm although this is still in the balance. Two 15 ton lifts *(18 × 10 m)*.

*Giuseppe Garibaldi*

**LEXINGTON** AVT 16
**BON HOMME RICHARD** CVA 31
**ORISKANY** CV 34

*Hancock/Intrepid classes ("Bon Homme Richard") 4/1960 (*L & L van Ginderen*)*

**Displacement, tons:** 29 600 light; 41 900 full load *(Bon Homme Richard)*. 28 200 light; 40 600 full load *(Oriskany)*. 29 783 light; 42 113 full load *(Lexington)*
**Length, feet (metres):** 899 *(274)* oa; 889 *(270.9) (Lexington)*
**Beam, feet (metres):** 103 *(31.4)* except *Oriskany* 106.5 *(32.5)*
**Draught, efet (metres):** 31 *(9.5)*
**Flight deck width, feet (metres):** 172 *(52.4) (B.H.R.) Lexington* 192 *(58.5)* and *Oriskany* 195 *(59.5)*
**Catapults:** 2 steam
**Aircraft:** 70 to 80 for CVA/CV type; none assigned to *Lexington*
**Guns:** 2—5 in *(127 mm)*/38 (single Mk 24) in *Oriskany;* 4 guns in *B.H.R.;* all removed from *Lexington*
**Main engines:** 4 geared turbines (Westinghouse); 4 shafts; 150 000 shp
**Boilers:** 8 Babcock & Wilcox
**Speed, knots:** 30+
**Complement:** CVA/CV type: 2 090 (110 officers, 1 980 enlisted men); plus approx 1 185 (135 officers, 1 050 enlisted men) in air wing for a total of approx 3 200 per ship. *Lexington:* 1 440 (75 officers, 1 365 enlisted men); no air unit assigned
**Commissioned:** 1943-50

These ships (formerly six including *Hancock* and *Intrepid*) originally were 'Essex' class aircraft carriers; extensively modernised during 1950s, being provided with enclosed bow, angled armoured flight deck, improved elevators, increased aviation fuel storage, and steam catapults. Construction of *Oriskany*, suspended after the Second World War, was completed in 1950 to a modified 'Essex' design.

*Bon Homme Richard* and *Oriskany* are laid up at Bremerton.

**Training Carrier:** *Lexington* (AVT 16) operates as a training ship and is based at Pensacola, Florida. The ship has no aircraft maintenance or arming capabilities, and is not considered as a combat ship. In an emergency, aircraft could be embarked on a very restricted operational basis. She is scheduled to serve in this capacity until 1992 when she will be relieved by *Coral Sea.*

**Modernisation:** These ships have been modernised under several programmes to increase their ability to operate more-advanced aircraft. Have angled flight deck. Three elevators fitted; 'Pointed' centreline lift forward between catapults, deck-edge lift on port side at leading edge of angled deck, and deck-edge lift on starboard side aft of island structure.

**INVINCIBLE** R 05
**ILLUSTRIOUS** R 06
**ARK ROYAL** R 07

**Displacement, tons:** 16 000 standard; 19 500 full load
**Dimensions, feet (metres):** 632 wl; 677 oa (685.8 *(Ark Royal)*) × 90 × 21(keel) × 26 (screws) *(192.8; 206.6 (209.1) × 27.5 × 6.4 × 8)*
**Width, feet (metres):** 105 oa *(31.9)*
**Flight deck length, feet (metres):** 550 *(167.8)*
**Aircraft:** (see notes)
**Missiles:** SAM; Twin Sea Dart (see notes)
**Guns:** 2 Phalanx; 2—20 mm (single) (see notes)
**Main engines:** 4 Rolls-Royce Olympus TM3B gas turbines; 2 shafts (reversible gear box); 94 000 shp
**Speed, knots:** 28
**Range, miles:** 5 000 at 18 knots
**Complement:** 670 plus 284 air group
**Commissioned:** 1977-85

The history of this class is a long and complex one starting in 1962. The first of class, the result of many compromises, was ordered from Vickers on 17 April 1973. At that time completion might have been expected in 1977-78 but changes in design and labour problems delayed this by two years. The order for the second ship, *Illustrious,* was placed on 14 May 1976, while the third, *Ark Royal,* was placed in December 1978. *Invincible* sea trials started May 1979 and *Ark Royal* 19 October 1984.

The primary task of this class, apart from providing a command centre for maritime air forces, is the operation of both helicopters and STOVL aircraft. Provision has been made for sufficiently large lifts and hangars to accommodate the next generation of both these aircraft.

The design allows for an open fo'c'sle head and a slightly angled deck which allows the Sea Dart launcher to be set almost amidships.
**Flight deck:** *Invincible* and *Illustrious* have been fitted with a 7 degree Ski-jump and *Ark Royal* has a 12 degree Ski-jump.
**Gunnery:** As a result of experience in the 1982 Falklands' campaign the two 20 mm Phalanx and two 20 mm GAM-BO1 (single) were fitted, the latter between the funnels, in the first two. Subsequently orders placed for three Goalkeeper systems per ship as replacements. *Ark Royal* has three Phalanx, one each on port quarter sponson, midships abreast the mainmast and at the bow. A third may be retrofitted in other pair.
**Missiles:** GWS 30 for Sea Dart. This also has a reasonable anti-ship capability. Sea Eagle for use on Sea Harriers. British Aerospace is conducting a study (completion December 1986) for fitting of four 4-barrelled Seawolf launchers with two Type 911 radar trackers.
**Refit:** In March 1986 *Invincible* paid off for long refit to last two years. To include a 12° Ski Jump, space for at least 22 aircraft (Sea Harriers, AEW Sea Kings and ASW helicopters), three Goalkeeper systems, new C3 systems and Type 996 3D radar if it is available in time.

Left: *Invincible class ("Invincible")*
*3/1979 (Royal Navy)*
*Overleaf*
Left: *Invincible class ("Ark Royal")*
*1984 (Royal Navy)*
Right: *Invincible class ("Illustrious")*
*12/1982 (L & L van Ginderen)*

**KITTY HAWK**          CV 63
**CONSTELLATION**       CV 64
**AMERICA**             CV 66
**JOHN F. KENNEDY**     CV 67

**Displacement, tons:** *Kitty Hawk:* 60 100 standard; 81 123 full load *Constellation:* 60 100 standard; 81 773 full load *America:* 60 300 standard; 79 724 full load *John F. Kennedy:* 61 000 standard; 80 941 full load

**Length, feet (metres):** *Kitty Hawk* and *Constellation:* 1 046 *(318.8) America:* 1 047.5 *(319.3) John F. Kennedy:* 1 052 *(320.7)*

**Beam, feet (metres):** 130 *(39.6)*

**Draught,feet (metres):** 37 *(11.3)*

**Flight deck width, feet (metres):** 252 *(76.9)*

**Catapults:** 4 steam

**Aircraft:** Approx 85

**Missiles:** 3 Basic Point Defence Missile System (BPDMS) launchers (Mk 29) with NATO Sea Sparrow missiles

**Guns:** 3—20 mm Phalanx Mk 16 CIWS

**Main engines:** 4 geared turbines (Westinghouse); 4 shafts; 280 000 shp

**Boilers:** 8 Foster-Wheeler

**Speed, knots:** 30+

**Complement:** *Kittyhawk* 3 161 (162 officers, 2 999 enlisted men) plus 2 480 air wing; Total: 5 641. *John F. Kennedy* 3 117 (162 officers, 2 955 enlisted men) plus 2 480 air wing; Total: 5 597

**Commissioned:** 1961-68

Above: *Kitty Hawk/John F Kennedy classes ("America") 9/1985 (*L & L van Ginderen*)*

Below: *Kitty Hawk/John F Kennedy classes ("Constellation") 2/1985 (*Dr. Giorgio Arra*)*

These ships were built to an improved 'Forrestal' design and are easily recognised by their island structure being set farther aft than the superstructure in the four 'Forrestal' class ships.

**Appearance:** Painted black between flight deck and bridge to mask jet exhaust stains.

**Design:** They have two deck-edge lifts forward of the superstructure, a third lift aft of the structure, and the port- side lift on the after quarter. This arrangement considerably improves flight deck operations. Four C13 catapults (with one C13-1 in each of later ships). *John F. Kennedy* and *America* have stern anchors as well as bow anchors because of their planned bow sonar domes (one on the stern in *America*). All have a small radar mast abaft the island.

**Service Life Extension Programme (SLEP):** These four ships are to undergo their Service Life Extension Programme overhauls and modernization on the following tentative schedule: *Kitty Hawk* January 1988-February 1991; *Constellation*, October 1990-November 1993; *America*, April 1996-May 1999; *Kennedy*, January 1999-February 2002.

| MIDWAY | CV 41 |
| CORAL SEA | CV 43 |

**Displacement, tons:** *Midway:* 51 000 standard; 64 002 full load *Coral Sea:* 52 500 standard; 65 241 full load
**Dimensions, feet (metres):** 979 × 121 × 35.3 *(298.4 × 36.9 × 10.8)*
**Flight deck width, feet (metres):** 238 *(72.5)* max
**Catapults:** 2 steam in *Midway* (C13); 3 in *Coral Sea* (C11)
**Aircraft:** Approx 75
**Missiles:** 2 Mk 25 Sea Sparrow launchers
**Guns:** 3—20 mm Mk 15 CIWS
**Main engines:** 4 geared turbines (Westinghouse); 4 shafts; 212 000 shp
**Boilers:** 12 Babcock & Wilcox
**Speed, knots:** 30+
**Complement:** 2 533 (133 officers, 2 400 enlisted men), plus 2 239 air wing; Total: 4 772
**Commissioned:** 1945-47

The original three carriers of this class were the largest US warships constructed during the Second World War.

*Midway* was homeported at Yokosuka, Japan, in October 1973; she is the only US aircraft carrier to be based overseas.

*Coral Sea* exchanged fleets from Indian Ocean to Atlantic with *Carl Vinson* between March and September 1983 by both carriers doing a round-the-world deployment. On arrival at Norfolk, Virginia she began a $189.5 million overhaul at Norfolk Naval Shipyard, completing January 1985. This included modifications to handle F/A-18 aircraft.

*Midway* is to receive similar modifications.

*Coral Sea* will relieve *Lexington* as training carrier when *George Washington* commissions in 1991.

*Midway* will remain as a deployable carrier until the turn of the century.

**Design:** All built to the same design with a standard displacement of 45 000 tons, full load displacement of 60 100 tons, and an overall length of 968 ft. They have been extensively modified since completion.

They were the first US aircraft carriers with an armoured flight deck and the first US warships with a designed width too large to enable them to pass through the Panama Canal.

**Modernisation:** Extensively modernised. Their main conversion (*Midway* 1955-57 and *Coral Sea* 1958-60) gave them angled flight decks, steam catapults, enclosed bows, new electronics, and new lift arrangement. Both now have one lift forward and one aft of island on starboard side and third lift outboard on port side aft.

*Midway*'s 1966-70 modernisation included widening the flight deck, provisions for handling newer aircraft, new catapults, new lifts and new electronics.

*Coral Sea* had an extensive refit in 1979 and a further refit in 1983-84 which included replacement of flight deck.

*Midway class ("Midway") 7/1981 (Dr. Giorgio Arra)*

| | |
|---|---|
| **NIMITZ** | CVN 68 |
| **DWIGHT D. EISENHOWER** | CVN 69 |
| **CARL VINSON** | CVN 70 |
| **THEODORE ROOSEVELT** | CVN 71 |
| **ABRAHAM LINCOLN** | CVN 72 |
| **GEORGE WASHINGTON** | CVN 73 |

**Displacement, tons:** 72 798 (CVN 68), 72 916 (rest) light; 81 600 standard; 90 944 (CVN 68), 91 487 (rest) full load
**Dimensions, feet (metres):** 1 040 pp; 1 092 × 134 × 37 *(317; 332.9 × 40.8 × 11.3)*
**Flight deck width, feet (metres):** 252 *(76.8)* (257 *(78.4)* CVN 71)
**Catapults:** 4 steam (C13-1)
**Aircraft:** 90+
**Missiles:** 3 Basic Point Defence Missile System (BPDMS) launchers with Sea Sparrow missiles (see notes)
**Guns:** See notes
**Main engines:** 4 geared steam turbines; 4 shafts; 260 000 shp
**Nuclear reactors:** 2 pressurised-water cooled (A4W/A1G)
**Speed, knots:** 30+
**Complement:** 3 204 (161 officers, 3 043 enlisted men) plus 2 480 assigned to air wing for a total of 5 684 per ship
**Commissioned:** 1975-c1991

The lead ship for this class and the world's second nuclear-powered aircraft carrier was ordered 9 years after the first such ship, *Enterprise* (CVN 65).

**Classification:** *Nimitz* and *Eisenhower* were ordered as attack aircraft carriers (CVAN): reclassified CVN on 30 June 1975. First two ships will be refitted with A/S control centre and facilities for A/S aircraft and helicopters for their new multi-mission role (attack/ASW). *Vinson* has, and subsequent ships will be completed with, these facilities.

**Gunnery:** It is planned to add three 20 mm Mk 16 CIWS in *Eisenhower* during her overhaul in 1985-87. These Phalanx were fitted in *Nimitz* 1983-84 overhaul. Follow-on ships will be completed with four CIWS.

**Missiles:** *Eisenhower* will have Mk 29 Sea Sparrow fitted during her 1985-87 overhaul in place of Mk 25 which were fitted in *Nimitz* during 1983-84 overhaul. Mk 115 MFCS in first two ships to be replaced by Mk 91. Mk 91 in the remainder.

*Nimitz class ("Carl Vinson")*
*10/1985 (*Dr. Giorgio Arra*)*

**PRINCIPE DE ASTURIAS** R 11

**Displacement, tons:** 14 700 full load
**Dimensions, feet (metres):** 642.9 × 80 × 29.8
(screws) *(196 × 24.4 × 9.1)*
**Flight deck, feet (metres):** 574 × 98 *(175 × 27)*
**Aircraft:** 20 (V/STOL and helicopters)
**Guns:** 4—Meroka 20 mm (12-barrels) CIWS
**Main engines:** 2 LM 2500 gas turbines; 1 shaft
(cp propeller); 46 400 shp
**Speed, knots:** 26
**Range, miles:** 7 500 at 20 knots
**Complement:** 791 (not including Flag, Staff and
Air Group)
**Commissioned:** due 1987

Basically to the US Navy Sea Control Ship design
she was ordered on 29 June 1977. Associated
US firms are Gibbs and Cox, Dixencast, Bath Iron
Works and Sperry S.M.; USA providing loan of
$150 million.

**Aircraft:** 12 degree Ski-jump fitted. Air
complement to be 6-8 AV-8B, 6-8 Sea Kings and
8-4 AB 212 helicopters.
  Searchwater radar ordered for some of the Sea
Kings.

*Principe de Asturias (*British
Aerospace*)*

**VITTORIO VENETO**                    C 550

**Displacement, tons:** 7 500 standard; 8 850 full load
**Dimensions, feet (metres):** 589 × 63.6 × 19.7 *(179.6 × 19.4 × 6)*
**Aircraft:** 9 AB 212 helicopters
**Missiles:** SSM; 4 Teseo launchers SAM; Terrier/Standard ER (est 40; twin launcher Mk 10; Aster system)
**Guns:** 8—3 in *(76 mm)*/62 (MMK single); 6—40 mm/70 (twin) Breda for Dardo systems
**A/S weapons:** 2 triple US Mk 32 for A/S torpedoes; helicopter torpedoes
**Main engines:** 2 Tosi double reduction geared turbines; 2 shafts; 73 000 shp
**Boilers:** 4 Foster-Wheeler type (Ansaldo); 711 psi *(50 kg/cm²)*; 842°F *(450°C)*
**Speed, knots:** 32
**Oil fuel, tons:** 1 200
**Range, miles:** 5 000 at 17 knots
**Complement:** 550 (50 officers, 500 men)
**Commissioned:** 1969

Developed from the 'Andrea Doria' class but with much larger helicopter squadron and improved facilities for anti- submarine operations. Projected under the 1959-60 New Construction Programme, but her design was recast several times. Started trials 30 April 1969. Fitted with two sets of stabilisers.

**Modernisation:** In hand from 1981-early 1984 for modernisation which included the four Teseo launchers and the three twin Breda Compact 40 mm.

*Vittorio Veneto, 1980 (*L & L van Ginderen*)*

**JEANNE D'ARC** (ex-*La Résolue*)     R 97

**Displacement, tons:** 10 000 standard; 12 365 full load
**Dimensions, feet (metres):** 597.1 × 78.7 hull × 24 *(182 × 24 × 7.3)*
**Flight deck, feet (metres):** 203.4 × 68.9 *(62 × 21)*
**Aircraft:** WG 13 Lynx helicopters (4 in peacetime as training ship; 8 in wartime)
**Missiles:** SSM; 6 Exocet MM 38 (single cells)
**Guns:** 4—3.9 in *(100 mm)* (single)
**Main engines:** Rateau-Bretagne geared turbines; 2 shafts; 40 000 shp
**Boilers:** 4; working pressure 640 psi *(45 kg/cm²)*; 842°F *(450°C)*
**Speed, knots:** 26.5
**Oil fuel, tons:** 1 360
**Range, miles:** 6 000 at 15 knots
**Complement:** 809 (30 officers, 587 ratings and 192 cadets)
**Commissioned:** 1964

Authorised under the 1957 estimates. Used for training officer cadets in peacetime. In wartime, after rapid modification, she would be used as a commando ship, helicopter carrier or troop transport with commando equipment and a battalion of 700 men. The lift has a capacity of 12 tons. The ship is almost entirely air-conditioned.

Operates with the Training Squadron for an autumn/spring cruise with summer refit. Belongs to Atlantic Fleet. Due to pay off in 2004.

*Jeanne d'Arc, 1981 (*French Navy*)*

| IOWA | BB 61 |
| NEW JERSEY | BB 62 |
| MISSOURI | BB 63 |
| WISCONSIN | BB 64 |

**Displacement, tons:** 45 000
standard; 58 000 full load
**Dimensions, feet (metres):** 887.2 ×
108.2 × 38 *(270.4 × 33 × 11.6) (New
Jersey* length 887.6 *(270.5))*
**Missiles:** SSM; 32 (8 quad launchers)
Tomahawk; 16 (4 quad) Harpoon
**Guns:** 9—16 in *(406 mm)*/50 (triple);
12—5 in *(127 mm)*/38 (twin Mk 38)
in *New Jersey* and *Iowa;* 20 in
*Missouri* and *Wisconsin;* 4 Mk 15
20 mm CIWS Phalanx *(New Jersey,
Iowa* and *Missouri)*; 20-40 mm
*(Missouri* only)
**Main engines:** 4 geared turbines
(General Electric in BB 61 and
BB 63; Westinghouse in BB 62 and
BB 64); 4 shafts; 212 000 shp
**Boilers:** 8 Babcock & Wilcox, 600 psi
**Speed, knots:** 35
**Oil fuel, tons:** 6 840
**Range, miles:** 5 000 at 30 knots;
15 000 at 17 knots
**Complement:** 1 537
**Commissioned:** 1943-44

*Iowa class ("New Jersey") 8/1985
(Dr. Giorgio Arra)*

These ships were the largest battleships ever built except for the Japanese *Yamato* and *Musashi* (64 170 tons standard, 863 ft *(263 m)* overall, nine 18.1 in guns). All four 'Iowa' class ships were in action in the Pacific during the Second World War. Three were 'mothballed' after the war with *Missouri* being retained in service as a training ship.

On 27 July 1981, *New Jersey* left Bremerton under tow for Long Beach Naval Shipyard, arriving 6 August 1981. She entered the shipyard on 1 October. *New Jersey* recommissioned on 28 December 1982 and joined the Pacific Fleet for duty. She began her first operational deployment in March 1983, was deployed off Central America and, later, off Lebanon.

On 13 July 1982 the contract for *Iowa's* reactivation/modernisation was signed jointly with Avondale Shipyards, Westwego, Louisiana and Ingalls Shipbuilding Corporation, Pascagoula, Mississippi. This dual agreement was necessary because Ingalls, the prime contractor, did not have a large dock for the ship. As a result she was docked by Avondale from 1 October 1982 to 30 January 1983. Under original plans *Iowa* was to recommission on 14 July 1984 but in December 1983 the need to relieve *New Jersey* in the Mediterranean caused a reprogramming. At a cost of $17.4 million ($4.5 million for changes to design and contract and $12.9 million to cover a two shift, 6 day week) the date was advanced to 8 April 1984.

In FY 1984, $57.7 million was approved for long lead items for *Missouri*, with an estimated additional $422.6 million required for completion. However, the ultimate overall cost of $467.3 million was realised from savings from competition for shipbuilding contracts, and no funds were included in the FY 1985 budget. *Missouri* activated at Long Beach Naval Shipyard, was completed in April 1986 for commissioning in July. In the FY 1986 budget, $469 million was approved for reactivation of *Wisconsin*. She is currently berthed at Philadelphia Naval Shipyard.

A contract for her activation is expected to be awarded in August, 1986 and activation will start in FY 1987.

**ANDREA DORIA**     C 553
**CAIO DUILIO**      C 554

**Displacement, tons:** 5 000 standard; 6 500 full load
**Dimensions, feet (metres):** 489.8 × 56.4 × 16.4 *(149.3 × 17.2 × 5)*
**Aircraft:** 4 AB 212 helicopters
**Missiles:** SAM; Terrier (est 32, twin launcher)
**Guns:** 8—3 in *(76 mm)*/62 (single MMK) (6 in *Caio Duilio*)
**A/S weapons:** 2 triple US Mk 32 torpedo tubes; helicopter torpedoes
**Main engines:** 2 double reduction geared turbines *(Doria,* CNR; *Duilio,* Ansaldo); 2 shafts; 60 000 shp
**Boilers:** 4 Foster-Wheeler 711 psi *(50 kg/cm²)* *(Duilio,* Ansaldo; *Doria,* CNR); 842°F *(450°C)*
**Speed, knots:** 31
**Range, miles:** 5 000 at 17 knots
**Oil fuel, tons:** 950
**Complement:** 470 (45 officers, 425 men)
**Commissioned:** 1964

Escort cruisers with a good helicopter capacity in relation to their size. *Enrico Dandolo* was the name originally allocated to *Andrea Doria*.

**Helicopter platform:** Helicopters operate from a platform aft measuring 98.5 × 52.5 ft *(30 × 16 m)*.

*Andrea Doria class ("Andrea Doria")*
*11/1985 (*G. Gyssels*)*

**BAINBRIDGE** CGN 25

**Displacement, tons:** 7 804 light; 8 592 full load
**Dimensions, feet (metres):** 565 × 57.9 × 25.4
  *(172.3 × 17.6 × 7.7)*
**Missiles:** SSM; 8 Harpoon (2 quad); SAM; 80
  Standard ER (SM-1) (2 twin Mk 10 launchers)
**Guns:** 2—20 mm Mk 16 Phalanx CIWS
**A/S weapons:** 1 ASROC 8-tube launcher; 2
  triple torpedo tubes (Mk 32)
**Main engines:** 2 geared turbines; 2 shafts;
  60 000 shp
**Nuclear reactors:** 2 pressurised-water cooled
  D2G (General Electric)
**Speed, knots:** 30
**Complement:** 566 (32 officers, 534 enlisted
  men)
**Flag accommodations:** 18 (6 officers, 12
  enlisted men)
**Commissioned:** 1962

*Bainbridge* was the US Navy's third nuclear-powered surface warship (after the cruiser *Long Beach* and the aircraft carrier *Enterprise*). Authorised in the FY 1959 shipbuilding programme. Construction cost was $163.61 million.

**Modernisation:** *Bainbridge* underwent an Anti-Air Warfare (AAW) modernisation at the Puget Sound Naval Shipyard from 30 June 1974 to 24 September 1976. The ship was fitted with the Naval Tactical Data System (NTDS) and improved guidance capability for missiles. Estimated cost of modernisation $103 million.

*Bainbridge class ("Bainbridge")
7/1981 (*Dr. Giorgio Arra*)

| | |
|---|---|
| **BELKNAP** | CG 26 |
| **JOSEPHUS DANIELS** | CG 27 |
| **WAINWRIGHT** | CG 28 |
| **JOUETT** | CG 29 |
| **HORNE** | CG 30 |
| **STERETT** | CG 31 |
| **WILLIAM H. STANDLEY** | CG 32 |
| **FOX** | CG 33 |
| **BIDDLE** | CG 34 |

**Displacement, tons:** 6 570 standard; 8 200 full load (CG 26-28); 8 065 (CG 29-33); 8 250 (CG 34)

**Dimensions, feet (metres):** 547 × 54.8 × 28.8 sonar; 19 keel *(166.7 × 16.7 × 8.8; 5.8)*

**Aircraft:** 1 SH-2D LAMPS helicopter

**Missiles:** SSM; 8 Harpoon (2 quad); Tomahawk to be fitted. SAM; 60 Standard ER/ASROC (1 twin Mk 10 launcher)

**Guns:** 1—5 in *(127 mm)*/54 (Mk 42) 2—20 mm Mk 16 CIWS Phalanx

**A/S weapons:** ASROC (see above); 2 triple torpedo tubes (Mk 32)

**Main engines:** 2 geared turbines (General Electric except De Laval in CG 29-31 and 33); 2 shafts; 85 000 shp

**Boilers:** 4 (Babcock & Wilcox in CG 26-28, 32-34; Combustion Engineering in CG 29-31)

**Speed, knots:** 32.5

**Complement:** 513 (25 officers, 488 enlisted men)

**Flag accommodations:** 18 (6 officers; 12 enlisted men) (CG 26)

**Commissioned:** 1964-67

*Belknap* was severely damaged in a collision with the carrier *John F. Kennedy* (CV 67) on 22 November 1975 near Sicily. Repair and modernisation began 9 January 1978. Estimated cost $213 million and included new improved 5 in gun, up-dated missile armament, sonar, communications and radar suites as well as improvements in habitability. Recommissioned 10 May 1980.

**Design:** Distinctive in having their single missile launcher forward and 5 in gun mount aft. This arrangement allowed missile stowage in the larger bow section and provided space aft of the superstructure for a helicopter hangar and platform. The reverse gun-missile arrangement is found in *Truxtun*.

*Belknap class ("Belknap") 9/1985 (Dr. Giorgio Arra)*

**CALIFORNIA** CGN 36
**SOUTH CAROLINA** CGN 37

**Displacement, tons:** 8 706 light; 9 561 standard; 10 450 full load (9 473, *South Carolina*)
**Dimensions, feet (metres):** 596 × 61 × 31.5 *(181.7 × 18.6 × 9.6)*
**Missiles:** SSM; 8 Harpoon (2 quad); SAM; 80 Standard MR (two single Mk 13 launchers) (see note)
**Guns:** 2—5 in *(127 mm)*/54 (single Mk 45); 2 Phalanx 20 mm Mk 16 CIWS
**A/S weapons:** 6 Mk 32 torpedo tubes (triple); 1 ASROC 8-tube launcher (Mk 16)
**Main engines:** 2 geared turbines; 2 shafts; 60 000 shp
**Nuclear reactors:** 2 pressurised-water cooled D2G (General Electric)
**Speed, knots:** 30+
**Complement:** 584 (30 officers, 554 enlisted men)
**Commissioned:** 1974-75

The construction of a third ship of this class (DLGN 38) was also authorised in FY 1968, but the rising costs of these ships and development of the DXGN/DLGN 38 design (now 'Virginia' class) caused the third ship to be cancelled.

**Design:** No helicopter support facilities provided.

**Missiles:** These ships carry 80 surface-to-air missiles divided equally between a magazine beneath each launcher. It is planned to fit Tomahawk missiles with armored-box launchers (ABL).

*California class ("California")*
*6/1977 (*C & S Taylor*)*

**COLBERT** C 611

**Displacement, tons:** 8 500 standard; 11 300 full load
**Dimensions, feet (metres):** 593.2 × 66.1 × 25.2 *(180.8 × 20.2 × 7.7)*
**Missiles:** SSM; 4 MM 38 Exocet (single); SAM; 48 Masurca (1 twin launcher) (see notes)
**Guns:** 2—3.9 in *(100 mm)* Model 68 single automatic; 12—57 mm in 6 twin mountings, 3 on each side
**Armour:** 50—80 mm belt and 50 mm deck
**Main engines:** 2 sets CEM-Parsons geared turbines; 2 shafts; 86 000 shp
**Boilers:** 4 Indret multi-tubular; 640 psi *(45 kg/cm²)*; 842°F *(450°C)*
**Speed, knots:** 31.5
**Oil fuel, tons:** 1 492
**Range, miles:** 4 000 at 25 knots
**Complement:** 560 (24 officers, 536 men)
**Commissioned:** 1959

She is equipped as command ship and for radar control of air strikes. Refitted mid-1981 to mid-1982. Serves as Flagship of the Mediterranean Fleet.

**Missiles:** *Colbert* carries Mk 2 Mod 3 semi-active radar homing version missiles for Masurca.

**Refit:** Further refit from August 1981 to November 1982 including improvements to *Masurca* (range extended to 20 miles (30 km), fitting of satellite communications, new cabling and improvements to accommodation. Operational spring 1983 with life extension until at least 1995.

*Colbert 6/1981 (*L & L van Ginderen*)*

| | |
|---|---|
| **LEAHY** | CG 16 |
| **HARRY E. YARNELL** | CG 17 |
| **WORDEN** | CG 18 |
| **DALE** | CG 19 |
| **RICHMOND K. TURNER** | CG 20 |
| **GRIDLEY** | CG 21 |
| **ENGLAND** | CG 22 |
| **HALSEY** | CG 23 |
| **REEVES** | CG 24 |

**Displacement, tons:** 4 650 light; 5 670 standard; 8 203 full load

**Dimensions, feet (metres):** 533 × 54.9 × 24.8 sonar; 19.6 keel *(162.5 × 16.6 × 7.6; 6)*

**Missiles:** SSM; 8 Harpoon (2 quad) SAM; 80 Standard ER (SM-2) (2 Mk 10 launchers)

**Guns:** 2—20 mm Mk 16 CIWS Phalanx

**A/S weapons:** 1 ASROC 8-tube launcher; 2 triple torpedo tubes (Mk 32)

**Main engines:** 2 geared turbines; 2 shafts; 85 000 shp

**Boilers:** 4 (Babcock & Wilcox in CG 16-20, Foster- Wheeler in 21-24)

**Speed, knots:** 32.7

**Fuel, tons:** 1 800

**Range, miles:** 8 000 at 20 knots

**Complement:** 513 (25 officers, 488 enlisted men)

**Flag accommodations:** 18 (6 officers, 12 enlisted men)

**Commissioned:** 1962-64

'Double-end' missile cruisers especially designed to screen fast carrier task forces.

**Design:** Distinctive in having twin missile launchers forward and aft with ASROC launcher between the forward missile launcher and bridge on main deck level.

There is a helicopter landing area aft but only limited support facilities are provided; no hangar.

*Leahy class ("Halsey") 12/1979*
*(*Dr. Giorgio Arra*)*

**LONG BEACH** CGN 9

**Displacement, tons:** 15 540 light; 17 525 full load
**Dimensions, feet (metres):** 721.2 × 73.2 × 29.7 *(219.9 × 22.3 × 9.1)*
**Aircraft:** Deck for utility helicopter
**Missiles:** SSM; 8 Harpoon (2 quad); 8 Tomahawk (2 quad) SAM; Terrier/Standard ER (2 twin Mk 10 launchers)
**Guns:** 2—5 in *(127 mm)*/38 (single Mk 30); 2 Phalanx Mk 16 CIWS
**A/S weapons:** 1 ASROC 8-tube launcher; 2 triple torpedo tubes (Mk 32)
**Main engines:** 2 geared turbines (General Electric); 2 shafts; 80 000 shp
**Nuclear reactors:** 2 pressurised-water cooled C1W (Westinghouse)
**Speed, knots:** 30
**Complement:** 825 (65 officers, 760 enlisted men)
**Flag accommodations:** 68 (10 officers, 58 enlisted men)
**Commissioned:** 1961

*Long Beach class ("Long Beach")*
*4/1983 (*Dr. Giorgio Arra*)*

*Long Beach* was the first ship to be designed as a cruiser for the USA since the end of the Second World War. She is the world's first nuclear-powered surface warship and the first warship to have a guided missile main battery.

**Engineering:** The reactors are similar to those of *Enterprise* (CVN 65). *Long Beach* first got underway on nuclear power on 5 July 1961. After four years of operation and having steamed more than 167 700 miles she underwent her first overhaul and refuelling at the Newport News Shipbuilding and Dry Dock Company from August 1965 to February 1966.

**Modernisation:** As a result of the 1976 cancellation of the planned fitting of AEGIS *Long Beach* underwent a mid-life modernisation. This included updating of missile systems, restoration of the missile radars, the SPS 32 and 33 air search replaced by SPS 48 and 49 systems, replacement of the ship's computer and modernisation of the communications system. Duration 6 October 1980 to 26 March 1983 at Puget Sound Naval Shipyard.

| | |
|---|---|
| **TICONDEROGA** | CG 47 |
| **YORKTOWN** | CG 48 |
| **VINCENNES** | CG 49 |
| **VALLEY FORGE** | CG 50 |
| **THOMAS S. GATES** | CG 51 |
| **BUNKER HILL** | CG 52 |
| **MOBILE BAY** | CG 53 |
| **ANTIETAM** | CG 54 |
| **LEYTE GULF** | CG 55 |
| **BENNINGTON** | CG 56 |

**Displacement, tons:** 9 600 full load
**Dimensions, feet (metres):** 565.8 × 55 × 31
*(172.5 × 16.8 × 9.5)*
**Aircraft:** 2 LAMPS I (CG 47, 48) III helicopters
**Missiles:** SSM; 8 Harpoon (quad launchers);
SAM/ASW; 88 Standard-ER (SM-2)/ASROC
(2 twin Mk 26 launchers) (see notes)
**Guns:** 2—5 in *(127 mm)*/54 (single Mk 45); 2—
20 mm/76 Phalanx (6-barrelled Mk 16 CIWS);
2—40 mm saluting guns
**A/S weapons:** ASROC; 6—Mk 32 torpedo tubes
(triple)
**Main engines:** 4 General Electric LM 2500 gas
turbines; 2 shafts; 80 000 shp
**Speed, knots:** 30+
**Complement:** 395 (37 officers, 358 enlisted
men)
**Commissioned:** 1983-88 (plus 3 building, 10
ordered and 8 projected)

The 'Ticonderoga' class fulfills the proposal for a
non-nuclear AEGIS armed ship as proposed in
the early 1970s, but subsequently dropped to
avoid conflict with the Navy's nuclear propelled
cruiser programme.

The original programme class force level was
18 which was increased to 24 in February 1980
and is now 27.

**Appearance:** *Vincennes* and later ships have a
tripod mainmast.

**Design:** The 'Ticonderoga' class design is a
modification of the 'Spruance' class. The same
basic hull is used, with the same gas turbine
propulsion plant although the overall length is
increased by the 3.6 ft *(1.1 m)* bulwark.

**Missiles:** From CG 52 onwards each ship will be
equipped with two Mk 41 vertical launchers (61
missiles per launcher) in place of Mk 26
launchers. Tomahawk will be carried in CG 52
onwards with 8 missiles in each VLS launcher
and 12 in the magazines.

*Ticonderoga class ("Vincennes")*
*1/1986 (*Dr. Giorgio Arra*)*

**TRUXTUN**  CGN 35

**Displacement, tons:** 8 322 light; 9 127 full load
**Dimensions, feet (metres):** 564 × 58 × 31 *(171.9 × 17.7 × 9.4)*
**Aircraft:** 1 helicopter
**Missiles:** SSM; 8 Harpoon (2 quad); SAM/ASW; 60 Standard ER/ASROC (1 twin Mk 10 launcher)
**Guns:** 1—5 in *(127 mm)*/54 (single Mk 42); 2 Phalanx 20 mm Mk 16 CIWS
**A/S weapons:** ASROC (see above); 4 fixed torpedo tubes (Mk 32)
**Main engines:** 2 geared turbines; 2 shafts; 60 000 shp
**Nuclear reactors:** 2 pressurised-water cooled D2G (General Electric)
**Speed, knots:** 30
**Complement:** 567 (31 officers, 536 enlisted men)
**Flag accommodations:** 18 (6 officers, 12 enlisted men)
**Commissioned:** 1967

*Truxtun* was the US Navy's fourth nuclear-powered surface warship. The Navy had requested seven oil-burning frigates in the FY 1962 shipbuilding programme; Congress authorised seven ships, but stipulated that one ship must be nuclear-powered.

Although the *Truxtun* design is adapted from the 'Belknap' class, the nuclear ship's gun-missile launcher arrangement is reversed from the non-nuclear ships.

**Name:** *Truxtun* is the fifth ship to be named after Commodore Thomas Truxton *(sic)* who commanded the frigate *Constellation* (38 guns) in her successful encounter with the French frigate *L'Insurgente* (44) in 1799.

*Truxtun class ("Truxtun") 3/1980*
*(Dr. Giorgio Arra)*

| | |
|---|---|
| VIRGINIA | CGN 38 |
| TEXAS | CGN 39 |
| MISSISSIPPI | CGN 40 |
| ARKANSAS | CGN 41 |

**Displacement, tons:** 8 623 light; 11 000 full load

**Dimensions, feet (metres):** 585 × 63 × 29.5
*(178.4 × 19.2 × 9)*

**Aircraft:** 2

**Missiles:** SSM; 8 Harpoon (2 quad); 8 Tomahawk (2 quad) SAM/ASW; Standard MR/ASROC (2 twin Mk 26 launchers)

**Guns:** 2—5 in *(127 mm)*/54 (single Mk 45); 2—20 mm Mk 16 CIWS in CGN 38 (being installed in remainder) 2—40 mm Mk 11 saluting guns

**A/S weapons:** ASROC (see above); 2 triple torpedo tubes (Mk 32)

**Main engines:** 2 geared turbines; 2 shafts; 100 000 shp

**Reactors:** 2 pressurised-water cooled D2G (General Electric)

**Speed, knots:** 30+

**Complement:** 562 (29 officers, 533 enlisted men)

**Commissioned:** 1976-80

**Design:** The principal differences between the 'Virginia' and 'California' classes are the provision of helicopters, with improvements to anti-air warfare capability, electronic warfare equipment, and anti-submarine fire control system. The deletion of the separate ASROC Mk 16 launcher permitted the 'Virginia' class to be 11 ft shorter.

**Helicopters:** A hangar for helicopters is installed beneath the fantail flight-deck with a telescoping hatch cover and an electro-mechanical elevator provided to transport helicopters between the main deck and hangar. These are the first US post-Second World War destroyer/cruiser ships with a hull hangar.

*Virginia class ("Arkansas") 8/1985*
*(Dr. Giorgio Arra)*

## GREECE

**MIAOULIS** (ex-USS *Ingraham*)        D 211

## TURKEY

**ZAFER** (ex-USS *Hugh Purvis*)        D 356

**Displacement, tons:** 2 200 standard; 3 320 full load
**Dimensions, feet (metres):** 376.5 × 40.9 × 19 *(114.8 × 12.5 × 5.8)*
**Aircraft:** 1 Alouette III helicopter
**Guns:** 6—5 in *(127 mm)*/38 (twin Mk 38); 6— 20 mm Rheinmetal S 20 (single); 2—12.7 mm MGs
**Missiles:** SAM; Portable Redeye
**A/S weapons:** 6—Mk 32 torpedo tubes (2 triple); 2 ahead throwing Hedgehogs
**Main engines:** 2 geared turbines; 2 shafts; 60 000 shp
**Boilers:** 4
**Speed, knots:** 34
**Range, miles:** 4 600 at 15 knots
**Complement:** 269 (16 officers, 94 POs, 159 men)
**Commissioned:** 1944

## GREECE

Former fleet destroyer of the 'Allen M. Sumner' class which had been modernised under the FRAM II programme.
Transferred by USA 16 July 1971 by sale.

## TURKEY

**Commissioned:** 1945

*Zafer* is of 'Allen M. Sumner' class of modified FRAM II having been used as a US Navy trials ship for planar passive sonar. There is an extra deckhouse on the hangar. Purchased 15 February 1973 after being on lease since 1 July 1972.

*Allen M Sumner class ("Miaoulis")*

**ARDITO**          D 550
**AUDACE**         D 551

**Displacement, tons:** 3 600 standard; 4 400 full
  load
**Dimensions, feet (metres):** 448 × 46.6 × 15.1
  *(136.6 × 14.2 × 4.6)*
**Aircraft:** 2 AB 212 helicopters
**Missiles:** SAM; Tartar/Standard (est 36; single
  launcher Mk 13)
**Guns:** 2—5 in *(127 mm)*/54 (single Compact);
  4—3 in *(76 mm)*/62 (single Compact)
**A/S weapons:** 2 triple US Mk 32 torpedo tubes;
  helicopter torpedoes
**Main engines:** 2 double reduction geared
  turbines (*Audace*—CNR, *Ardito*—Ansaldo); 2
  shafts; 73 000 shp
**Boilers:** 4 Foster-Wheeler type
**Speed, knots:** 34
**Range, miles:** 3 000 at 20 knots
**Complement:** 380 (30 officers, 350 men)
**Commissiooned:** 1972

It was announced in April 1966 that two new
guided missile destroyers would be built. They
are basically similar to, but an improvement in
design on that of the 'Impavido' class. Both fitted
with stabilisers.

*Audace class ("Audace") 1980 (*L & L
van Ginderen*)*

**BRISTOL**                          D 23

**Displacement, tons:** 6 300 standard; 7 100 full
  load
**Dimensions, feet (metres):** 490 wl; 507 oa × 55 ×
  16.8 (23 sonar dome) *(149.3; 154.5 × 16.8 × 5.2
  (7))*
**Aircraft:** Landing platform for 1 Wasp helicopter
**Missiles:** SAM; Sea Dart (twin launcher) (40
  missiles)
**Guns:** 1—4.5 in *(115 mm)/*55 (Mk 8); 4—30 mm
  BMARC (twin); 2—20 mm Oerlikon (single); 2—
  20 mm GAM-BO1 (single)
**Main engines:** COSAG; 2 Standard Range geared
  steam turbines, 30 000 shp; 2 Bristol-Siddeley
  Marine Olympus TM1A gas turbines, 30 000
  shp; 2 shafts
**Boilers:** 2
**Speed, knots:** 28
**Fuel, tons:** 900
**Range, miles:** 5 000 at 18 knots
**Complement:** 397 (30 officers, 367 ratings)
**Commissioned:** 1973

Designed around Sea Dart GWS 30 weapons
system. Fitted with Action Data Automation
Weapon System. Started trials 10 April 1972.
Remainder of class cancelled owing to high cost
and cancellation of aircraft-carrier building
programme for which they were intended as
escorts. Officially listed as 'destroyer' which is
presumably as the result of her Sea Dart area
defence capability and despite the lack of a
helicopter.
  Fitted with flagship facilities in 1979-80 refit.
Further refit 1984, completed March 1986.

*Bristol, 3/1981 (*Michael D. J.
Lennon*)*

**ACONIT**                                    D 609

**Displacement, tons:** 3 500 standard; 3 900 full
load
**Dimensions, feet (metres):** 416.7 × 44 × 18.9
*(127 × 13.4 × 5.8)*
**Missiles:** SSM; 4 MM 40 Exocet (see *Missile*
note)
**Guns:** 2—3.9 in *(100 mm)* (single)
**A/S weapons:** 1 Malafon launcher; 2 launchers
for Mk L5 torpedoes
**Main engines:** 1 Rateau geared turbine; 1 shaft;
28 650 shp
**Boilers:** 2 automatic 842°F *(450°C)*
**Speed, knots:** 27
**Range, miles:** 5 000 at 18 knots
**Complement:** 228 (15 officers, 213 men)
**Commissioned:** 1973

Forerunner of the F 67 Type. A one-off class
ordered under 1965 programme. In the Atlantic
Fleet. Due to pay off in 1999.

**Missiles:** In 1984 the A/S 12 in *(305 mm)* mortar
was replaced by 4 MM 40 launchers, with space
and weight for 4 more in future.

*Type C 65 ("Aconit") 9/1985 (*L & L
van Ginderen*)*

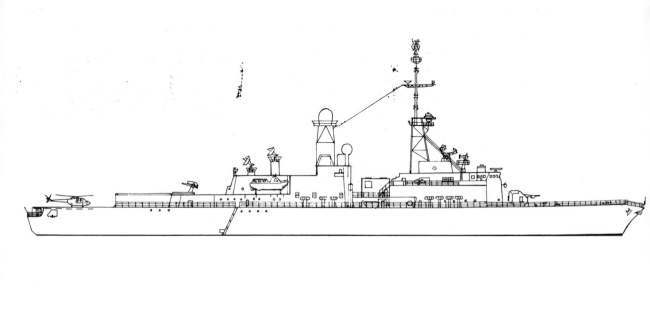

| | |
|---|---|
| **CASSARD** | D 614 |
| **JEAN BART** | D 615 |
| **COURBET** | D 616 |

**Displacement, tons:** 4 300 full load
**Dimensions, feet (metres):** 455.9 × 45.9 × 18.7
  *(139 × 14 × 5.7)*
**Aircraft:** Dauphin helicopter with hangar
**Missiles:** SSM; 8 MM 40; SAM; 1—Mk 13
  mounting for Standard SM1 MR (40 missiles)
  (see notes) 2 Sadral PDMS (either side of
  hangar)
**Guns:** 1—3.9 in *(100 mm)* Model 68 Compact
  Gun; 2—20 mm
**A/S weapons:** 2 fixed launchers for L5
  torpedoes (10 carried)
**Main engines:** 4 SEMT-Pielstick 18PA6 BTC
  'diesels rapides'; 2 shafts; 42 400 hp
**Speed, knots:** 29
**Range, miles:** 8 000 at 17 knots; 4 800 at 24
  knots
**Complement:** 240 (accommodation for 250)
**Commissioned:** 1988-1993 (4th vessel due
  1994)

On the same hull as the C 70 (A/S) a very
different armament and propulsion system is
being introduced.

**Missile launchers:** SAM launchers will be
refitted Mk 13 launchers from the T 47 (DDG)
ships, but VLS SAM with SM2 will be installed in
second pair.

*Type C 70 anti-aircraft version*

| | |
|---|---|
| **GEORGES LEYGUES** | D 640 |
| **DUPLEIX** | D 641 |
| **MONTCALM** | D 642 |
| **JEAN DE VIENNE** | D 643 |
| **PRIMAUGUET** | D 644 |
| **LAMOTTE PICQUET** | D 645 |

**Displacement, tons:** 3 830 standard; 4 170 full load
**Dimensions, feet (metres):** 455.9 × 45.9 × 18.7 *(139 × 14 × 5.7)*
**Aircraft:** Two WG 13 Lynx helicopters with Mk 46 torpedoes
**Missiles:** SSM; 4 MM 38 Exocet (MM 40 from *Montcalm* on) SAM; 26 Crotale EDIR, 1 launcher (see *Class* note)
**Guns:** 1—3.9 in *(100 mm)*; 2—20 mm
**A/S weapons:** 2 fixed launchers for L5 torpedoes (10 carried)
**Main engines:** CODOG; 2 Rolls-Royce Olympus gas turbines; 52 000 bhp; 2 SEMT-Pielstick 16PA6 CV280 diesels; 10 400 bhp; 2 shafts; cp screws
**Speed, knots:** 30 (18 on diesels)
**Range, miles:** 9 500 at 18 knots on diesels
**Complement:** 216 (15 officers, 201 men) (billets for 250)
**Commissioned:** 1979-88 (plus one on order)

**Class:** The first four of this class are the C 70(1) class. *Primauguet* fitted with towed array (DSBV 61) in place of DUBV 43, with a new Crotale Naval EDIR system combining extra range with an anti-missile capability (which is being retrofitted in first four from end 1985), possibly the new 100 mm Compact and Vampir Infra-Red Surveillance. The bridge will be raised one deck to overcome present problems.

**Helicopter:** The Lynx, as well as its A/S role, can have an anti-surface role when armed with four AS 12 missiles.

*Type C 70 (ASW) ("Georges Leygues") 10/1981 (*Dr. Giorgio Arra*)*

**ALCITEPE** (ex-USS *Robert A.*
  *Owens*)                                     D 346
**ANITTEPE** (ex-USS *Carpenter*)              D 347

**Displacement, tons:** 2 425 standard; 3 540 full
  load
**Dimensions, feet (metres):** 390.5 × 41 × 20.9
  *(119 × 12.5 × 6.4)*
**Guns:** 2—5 in *(127 mm)*/38 (twin Mk 38); 2—3 in
  *(76 mm)* (twin) (*Anittepe* only—aft); 2—35 mm
  (twin)
**A/S weapons:** 1 ASROC 8-tube launcher; 6 Mk
  32 torpedo tubes (triple)
**Main engines:** 2 geared turbines (General
  Electric); 2 shafts; 60 000 shp
**Boilers:** 4 Babcock & Wilcox
**Speed, knots:** 33
**Complement:** 275 (15 officers, 260 ratings)
**Commissioned:** 1949

*Anittepe* transferred 1981, *Alcitepe* in 1982.

*Carpenter class ("Anittepe") 9/1982*
*(Selim Sam)*

| | |
|---|---|
| **CHARLES F. ADAMS** | DDG 2 |
| **JOHN KING** | DDG 3 |
| **LAWRENCE** | DDG 4 |
| **CLAUDE V. RICKETTS** | DDG 5 |
| **BARNEY** | DDG 6 |
| **HENRY B. WILSON** | DDG 7 |
| **LYNDE McCORMICK** | DDG 8 |
| **TOWERS** | DDG 9 |
| **SAMPSON** | DDG 10 |
| **SELLERS** | DDG 11 |
| **ROBISON** | DDG 12 |
| **HOEL** | DDG 13 |
| **BUCHANAN** | DDG 14 |
| **BERKELEY** | DDG 15 |
| **JOSEPH STRAUSS** | DDG 16 |
| **CONYNGHAM** | DDG 17 |
| **SEMMES** | DDG 18 |
| **TATTNALL** | DDG 19 |
| **GOLDSBOROUGH** | DDG 20 |
| **COCHRANE** | DDG 21 |
| **BENJAMIN STODDERT** | DDG 22 |
| **RICHARD E. BYRD** | DDG 23 |
| **WADDELL** | DDG 24 |

*Charles F Adams class ("Henry B Wilson") 1/1986 (*Dr. Giorgio Arra*)*

**Displacement, tons:** 3 370 standard; 4 500 full load
**Dimensions, feet (metres):** 437 × 47 × 20 sonar/screws; 15.6 keel *(133.2 × 14.3 × 6.1; 4.8)*
**Missiles:** SSM; Harpoon (except in DDG 3, 8, 12, 21 and 23) SAM; Tartar (1 twin Mk 11 launcher) (DDG 2-14) SAM; Tartar (1 single Mk 13 launcher) (DDG 15-24)
**Guns:** 2—5 in *(127 mm)*/54 (single Mk 42)
**A/S weapons:** 1 ASROC 8-tube launcher; 2 triple torpedo tubes (Mk 32)
**Main engines:** 2 geared steam turbines (General Electric in DDG 2, 3, 7, 8, 10-13, 15-22; Westinghouse in DDG 4-6, 9, 14, 23, 24); 2 shafts; 70 000 shp
**Boilers:** 4 (Babcock & Wilcox in DDG 2, 3, 7, 8, 10-13, 20-22; Foster-Wheeler in DDG 4-6, 9, 14, 23, 24; Combustion Engineering in DDG 15-19)
**Speed, knots:** 30
**Complement:** 384 (21 officers, 363 enlisted men)
**Commissioned:** 1960-64

**Design:** These ships were built to an improved 'Forrest Sherman' class design with aluminium superstructures. DDG 20-24 have stem anchors because of sonar arrangement.

Several ships have been modified with an extension of the bridge structure on the starboard side on the 02 level.

**LÜTJENS** (ex-US *DDG 28*)  D 185
**MÖLDERS** (ex-US *DDG 29*)  D 186
**ROMMEL** (ex-US *DDG 30*)  D 187

**Displacement, tons:** 3 370 standard; 4 500 full load
**Dimensions, feet (metres):** 437 × 47 × 20 *(133.2 × 14.3 × 6.1)*
**Missiles:** SSM; Harpoon (quad) (see notes) SAM; 40 Tartar (single Mk 13) (see notes)
**Guns:** 2—5 in *(127 mm)*/54 (single Mk 42)
**A/S weapons:** 8 A/S ASROC rockets (octuple launcher); 6 Mk 32 torpedo tubes (2 triple); 1 DCT
**Main engines:** Geared steam turbines; 2 shafts; 70 000 shp
**Boilers:** 4 Combustion Engineering; 1 200 psi *(84.4 kg/cm²)*
**Speed, knots:** 30+
**Oil fuel, tons:** 900
**Range, miles:** 4 500 at 20 knots
**Complement:** 337 (19 officers, 318 men)
**Commissioned:** 1969-70

Modified to suit Federal German requirements and practice. 1965 contract.

**Appearance:** Some differences from 'Charles F. Adams' in W/T aerials and general outline, particularly the funnels.

**Missiles:** The Tartar missiles were replaced by Standard MR during the modernisation to Type 103A in 1974-76.
    The single-arm missile launcher being installed in Type 103B modernisation from 1983-86 is capable of firing Harpoon SSM and Standard MR SAM. Mixed missile magazine provided for 40 weapons.

**Modernisation:** The Type 103B modernisation and other modifications up to 1987 include:
(a) Replacement of SAM launcher by one single-arm Mk 13 launcher.
(b) Installation of two RAM-ASDM launchers.
(c) Improved fire control with digital in place of analog computers.
(d) Higher bridge with SPG 60 and SPQ 9 on a mast platform.
To be carried out by Naval Arsenal, Kiel and Howaldtswerke, Kiel: *Mölders* completed 29 March 1984; *Rommel* started December 1983, completion 26 July 1985; *Lütjens* started May 1985, completion December 1986.

*Modified Charles F Adams class ("Mölders") 5/1984 (*L & L van Ginderen*)*

| | |
|---|---|
| **FARRAGUT** | DDG 37 |
| **LUCE** (ex-*Dewey*) | DDG 38 |
| **MACDONOUGH** | DDG 39 |
| **COONTZ** | DDG 40 |
| **KING** | DDG 41 |
| **MAHAN** | DDG 42 |
| **DAHLGREN** | DDG 43 |
| **WILLIAM V. PRATT** | DDG 44 |
| **DEWEY** | DDG 45 |
| **PREBLE** | DDG 46 |

**Displacement, tons:** 4 150/4 580 standard; 6 150 full load

**Dimensions, feet (metres):** 512.5 × 52.5 × 23.4 sonar; 15 keel *(156.3 × 16 × 7.1; 4.6)*

**Missiles:** SSM; 8 Harpoon (quad) (not in DDG 38 and 41); SAM; Standard ER (SM-2) (1 twin Mk 10 launcher)

**Gun:** 1—5 in *(127 mm)*/54 (Mk 42)

**A/S weapons:** 1 ASROC 8-tube launcher; 2 triple torpedo tubes (Mk 32)

**Main engines:** 2 geared turbines; 2 shafts; 85 000 shp

**Boilers:** 4 (Foster-Wheeler in DDG 37-39; Babcock & Wilcox in DDG 40-46)

**Speed, knots:** 33

**Fuel, tons:** 900

**Range, miles:** 5 000 at 20 knots

**Complement:** 467 (27 officers, 440 enlisted men)

**Flag accommodations:** 19 (7 officers, 12 enlisted men)

**Commissioned:** 1959-61

**Conversion:** *Mahan* is trials ship for the New Threat Upgrade (NTU) system which includes SPS 48E (3D radar), SPS 49(V)5 (2D) radar, SYS 2 computerised AIO system and Standard SM-2ER missiles. This is the fit planned for all surface combatants from the early 1990s.

**Design:** These ships were the only US guided missile 'frigates' with separate masts and funnels. They have aluminium superstructures to reduce weight and improve stability. Early designs for this class had a second 5 in gun mount in the 'B' position; design revised when ASROC launcher was developed.

Helicopter landing area on stern, but no hangar and limited support capability.

*Coontz class ("Farragut") 11/1978*
*(US Navy)*

| GLAMORGAN | D 19 |
| FIFE | D 20 |

**Displacement, tons:** 5 440 standard; 6 200 full
load
**Dimensions, feet (metres):** 505 wl; 520.5 oa ×
54 × 20.5 (screws) (16.5 keel) *(153.9; 158.7 ×
16.5 × 6.3 (5))*
**Aircraft:** 1 Lynx HAS 2 helicopter
**Missiles:** SSM; 4 Exocet (single cells) SAM;
Seaslug (twin launcher aft) (36 missiles)
(*Glamorgan* only) Seacat (two quad launchers)
(*Fife* only)
**Guns:** 2—4.5 in *(115 mm)*/45 (twin Mk 6); 2—40
mm (*Glamorgan* only); 2—20 mm (single)
**A/S weapons:** 6 (2 triple) STWS torpedo tubes
**Main engines:** COSAG; 2 sets geared steam
turbines, 30 000 shp; 4 gas turbines, 30 000
shp; 2 shafts
**Boilers:** 2 Babcock & Wilcox
**Speed, knots:** 30; 25 on steam
**Fuel, tons:** 700
**Complement:** 472 (34 officers and 438 men)
**Commissioned:** 1966

*Glamorgan* hit by an Exocet missile on 12 June
1982 off the Falkland Islands, damaged and
subsequently repaired.
After lengthy refit *Fife* recommissioned March
1983—similar to *Glamorgan's* 1978-80 refit—
and serves as training ship for BRNC Dartmouth.

*County class ("Fife") 7/1979 (*L & L
van Ginderen*)*

| IROQUOIS | 280 |
|----------|-----|
| HURON | 281 |
| ATHABASKAN | 282 |
| ALGONQUIN | 283 |

**Displacement, tons:** 4 700 full load
**Dimensions, feet (metres):** 398 wl; 426 oa × 50 ×
   15.5 keel/ 21.5 screws *(121.4;129.8 × 15.2 ×*
   *4.7/6.6)*
**Aircraft:** 2 Sea King CHSS-2 A/S helicopters
**Missiles:** SAM; Sea Sparrow, 2 quad launchers
**Gun:** 1—5 in *(127 mm)/*54 OTO Melara Compact
**A/S weapons:** 1 Mk 10 Limbo; 2 triple Mk 32
   torpedo tubes
**Main engines:** Gas turbine; 2 Pratt & Whitney
   FT4A2; 50 000 shp; 2 Pratt & Whitney
   FT12AH3; 7 400 shp for cruising; 2 shafts
**Speed, knots:** 29 +
**Range, miles:** 4 500 at 20 knots
**Complement:** 245 (20 officers, 225 men) plus air
   unit, (7 officers + 33 men)
**Commissioned:** 1972-73

Designed as anti-submarine ships, they are fitted
with variable depth and hull sonar, landing deck
equipped with double hauldown and Beartrap,
flume type anti-rolling tanks to stabilise the ships
at low speed, pre-wetting system to counter
radio- active fallout, enclosed citadel, and bridge
control of machinery.

**Modernisation:** Announced in autumn 1983 that
this class would be modernised under TRUMP.
$650 million programme awarded to Davie S.B.
Co, Lauzon. During TRUMP, HSA WM 20 WCS,
medium range SAM, ASWDS, and OTO Melara
76 mm gun to be fitted. First ship to start late
1986 and last to complete 1991.

*DD 280 class ("Algonquin") 5/1986*

**DUPERRÉ**                    D 633

**Displacement, tons:** 2 800 standard; 3 900 full
  load
**Dimensions, feet (metres):** 435.7 × 41.7 × 20
  *(132.8 × 12.7 × 6.1)*
**Aircraft:** One WG 13 Lynx helicopter
**Missiles:** SSM; 4 Exocet MM 38 (single
  launchers)
**Gun:** 1—3.9 in *(100 mm)*
**A/S weapons:** Launcher for 8 torpedoes (Mk L5)
**Main engines:** 2 sets Rateau geared turbines; 2
  shafts; 63 000 shp
**Boilers:** 4 A & C de B Indret; 500 psi *(35 kg/cm²)*;
  617°F *(380°C)*
**Speed, knots:** 32
**Oil fuel, tons:** 800
**Range, miles:** 5 000 at 18 knots
**Complement:** 272 (15 officers, 257 men)
**Commissioned:** 1957

After serving as trial ship from 1967-71, she was
converted at Brest to her present state in 1972-
74 including an improved ASW control and
flagship facilities. Recommissioned 21 May 1974
and served as flagship Atlantic Fleet. On Friday
13 January 1978 she grounded heavily off Brest
and was severely damaged. Taken to Brest Navy
Yard for repairs. Completion February 1980 after
sea trials starting 3 December 1979. Has had
both main propulsion and electrical equipment
replaced. Serves in Mediterranean Fleet. Due for
deletion in 1990.

*Duperre 6/1975 (Dr. Giorgio Arra)*

TOURVILLE                   D 610
DUGUAY-TROUIN               D 611
DE GRASSE                   D 612

**Displacement, tons:** 4 580 standard; 5 745 full load

**Dimensions, feet (metres):** 501.3 × 50.2 × 18.7 *(152.8 × 15.3 × 5.7)*

**Aircraft:** Two WG 13 Lynx ASW helicopters

**Missiles:** SSM; 6 Exocet MM 38 (single launchers); SAM; Crotale S-A (see note)

**Guns:** 1—3.9 in *(100 mm)*; 2—20 mm (single)

**A/S weapons:** 1 Malafon rocket/homing torpedo launcher (13 missiles); 2 mountings for Mk L5 torpedoes (10 torpedoes)

**Main engines:** Rateau geared turbines; 2 shafts; 54 400 shp

**Boilers:** 4 automatic

**Speed, knots:** 32

**Range, miles:** 5 000 at 18 knots

**Complement:** 292 (17 officers, 275 men)

**Commissioned:** 1974-77

Developed from the 'Aconit' design. Originally rated as corvettes but reclassified as frigates on 8 July 1971 and given D pennant numbers like destroyers. *De Grasse* completed major refit September 1981.

**Missiles:** Octuple Crotale fitted in place of after 100 mm gun, *Duguay-Trouin* in 1979, *Tourville* in 1980 and *De Grasse* 1981.
  All to receive Crotale Naval EDIR.

*Type F 67 ("Duguay-Trouin")*
*9/1985 (L & L van Ginderen)*

## GREECE

| | |
|---|---|
| **ASPIS** (ex-USS *Conner)* | D 06 |
| **VELOS** (ex-USS *Charette)* | D 16 |
| **KIMON** (ex-FGS *Z 3,* | |
| ex-USS *Wadsworth)* | D 42 |
| **LONCHI** (ex--USS *Hall)* | D 56 |
| **NEARCHOS** (ex-FGS *Z 2,* | |
| ex-USS *Ringold)* | D 65 |
| **SFENDONI** (ex-USS *Aulick)* | D 85 |

## SPAIN

| | |
|---|---|
| **ALMIRANTE FERRANDIZ** | |
| (ex-USS *David W. Taylor)* | D 22 |
| **ALMIRANTE VALDES** | |
| (ex-USS *Converse)* | D 23 |
| **ALCALA GALIANO** | |
| (ex-USS *Jarvis)* | D 24 |
| **JORGE JUAN** | |
| (ex-USS *McGowan)* | D 25 |

## TURKEY

| | |
|---|---|
| **ISTANBUL** (ex-USS *Clarence K.* | |
| *Bronson)* | D 340 |
| **IZMIR** (ex-USS *Van* | |
| *Valkenburgh)* | D 341 |

*Fletcher class ("Almirante Valdes")*
*6/1983 (*G. Gyssels*)*

**Displacement, tons:** 2 050 standard; 3 050 full load
**Dimensions, feet (metres):** 376.5 × 39.5 × 18 *(114.7 × 12 × 5.5)*
**Guns:** 4—5 in *(127 mm)*/38; 6—3 in *(76 mm)*/55 (twin Mk 33); 2—12.7 MGs (06, 16, 56, 85)
**Missiles:** SAM; Portable Redeye
**A/S weapons:** Hedgehogs; DCs; 6 Mk 32 (triple) torpedo tubes in 16 and 85
**Torpedo tubes:** 5—21 in *(533 mm)* (quin), in 06, 16, 56 and 85
**Torpedo racks:** Side-launching for A/S torpedoes
**Main engines:** 2 sets GE geared turbines; 2 shafts; 60 000 shp
**Boilers:** 4 Babcock & Wilcox
**Speed, knots:** 32
**Range, miles:** 6 000 at 15 knots; 1 260 at full power
**Oil fuel, tons:** 506
**Complement:** 250
**Commissioned:** 1942-43

## GREECE

Transferred from USA, *Aspis, Lonchi* and *Velos* at Long Beach, California, on 15 September 1959, 9 February 1960 and 15 June 1959, respectively, *Sfendoni* at Philadelphia on 21 August 1959. All purchased 25 April 1977.

**Modernisation:** In May 1985 announced that three of this class are to be modernised by Selenia, Italy with modern electronic equipment. Two to be ex-US and one ex-FDR.

## SPAIN

**Commissioned:** 1943

All purchased from the USA on 1 October 1972. All will probably be deleted from 1986.

## TURKEY

**Commissioned:** 1943-44

*Istanbul* transferred 14 January 1967, *Izmir* 28 February 1967.

| DECATUR | DDG 31 |
| JOHN PAUL JONES | DDG 32 |
| SOMERS | DDG 34 |

**Displacement, tons:** 4 150 full load
**Dimensions, feet (metres):** 418.4 × 44 × 14.5 keel *(127.5 × 13.4 × 4.4)*
**Missiles:** SAM; Tartar (1 single Mk 13 launcher)
**Gun:** 1—5 in *(127 mm)*/54 (Mk 42)
**A/S weapons:** 1 ASROC 8-tube launcher; 2 triple torpedo tubes (Mk 32)
**Main engines:** 2 geared turbines (Westinghouse in *John Paul Jones* and *Decatur*; General Electric in *Somers*); 2 shafts; 70 000 shp
**Boilers:** 4 (Foster-Wheeler in *Decatur;* Babcock & Wilcox in *John Paul Jones* and *Somers*)
**Speed, knots:** 31 knots
**Fuel, tons:** 500
**Range, miles:** 4 500 at 20 knots
**Complement:** 337 (22 officers, 315 enlisted men) *(Decatur* and *John Paul Jones)*; 364 (25 officers and 339 enlisted men) *(Somers)*
**Commissioned:** 1956-59

'Forrest Sherman' and 'Hull' class destroyers that have been converted to a guided missile configuration. Plans for additional DDG conversions of this type were dropped. *Decatur* was reclassified as DDG 31 on 15 September 1966; *John Paul Jones* and *Somers* became DDG on 15 March 1967.

Due to increasing engineering difficulties, centring around the 1 200 psi plant, all the ships of the 'Forrest Sherman' and 'Hull' classes (both DDG and DD) (except DD 946) have been decommissioned.

*Forrest Sherman/Hull Classes (DDG) ("Somers") 1985. (*Dr Giorgio Arra*)*

| | |
|---|---|
| **FORREST SHERMAN** | DD 931 |
| **BIGELOW** | DD 942 |
| **MULLINNIX** | DD 944 |
| **EDSON** | DD 946 |
| **TURNER JOY** | DD 951 |

ANTI-SUBMARINE MODERNISATION

| | |
|---|---|
| **DAVIS** | DD 937 |
| **MANLEY** | DD 940 |
| **DUPONT** | DD 941 |
| **BLANDY** | DD 943 |
| **MORTON** | DD 948 |
| **RICHARD S. EDWARDS** | DD 950 |

**Displacement, tons:** 2 800/3 000 standard; 3 960/4 200 full load

**Dimensions, feet (metres):** 418 × 45 × 23 sonar; 14.5 keel *(127.4 × 13.7 × 7; 4.4)*

**Guns:** A/S Mod and DD 931; 2—5 in *(127 mm)*/54 (single Mk 42) Others; 3—5 in *(127 mm)*/54 (single Mk 42);

**A/S weapons:** 2 triple torpedo tubes (Mk 32); 1 ASROC 8-tube launcher in A/S modified ships

**Main engines:** 2 geared turbines (Westinghouse in DD 931, 937; General Electric in others); 2 shafts; 70 000 shp

**Boilers:** 4 Babcock & Wilcox (Foster-Wheeler in DD 937, 940-942)

**Speed, knots:** 33

**Oil fuel, tons:** 750

**Range, miles:** 4 500 at 20 knots

**Complement:** 292 (17 officers, 275 enlisted men) in unmodified ships; 304 in A/S mod ships (17 officers, 287 enlisted men)

**Commissioned:** 1955-59

These ships were the first US destroyers of post-Second World War design and construction to be completed with the DD designation. Four have been converted to a guided missile configuration (DDGs) and are listed separately.

**Modernisation:** Six ships of this class were extensively modified in 1967-71 to improve their anti-submarine capabilities.

During modernisation anti-submarine torpedo tubes were installed forward of bridge (on 01 level), deckhouse aft of second funnel was extended to full width of ship, ASROC launcher installed in place of after gun mounts on 01 level, and variable depth sonar fitted at stern. Six ships of this class were not modernised because of increased costs.

Above: *Forrest Sherman/Hull classes (DD) ("Turner Joy")*

Below: *Forrest Sherman/Hull classes (DD) ("Dupont") 3/1981 (*US Navy*)*

## GREECE

| | |
|---|---|
| **THEMISTOCLES** | |
| (ex-USS *Frank Knox*) | D 210 |
| **KANARIS** | |
| (ex-USS *Stickell*) | D 212 |
| **KOUNTOURIOTIS** | |
| (ex-USS *Rupertus*) | D 213 |
| **SACHTOURIS** | |
| (ex-USS *Arnold J. Isbell*) | D 214 |
| **TOMPAZIS** | |
| (ex-USS *Gurke*) | D 215 |
| **APOSTOLIS** | |
| (ex-USS *Charles P. Cecil*) | D 216 |
| **KRIEZIS** | |
| (ex-USS *Corry*) | D 217 |

## SPAIN (FRAM I)

| | |
|---|---|
| **CHURRUCA** (ex-USS *Eugene A.* | |
| *Greene*) | D 61 |
| **GRAVINA** (ex-USS *Furse*) | D 62 |
| **MENDEZ NUNTEZ** | |
| (ex-USS *O'Hare*) | D 63 |
| **LANGARA** (ex-USS *Leary*) | D 64 |
| **BLAS DE LEZO** | |
| (ex-USS *Noa*) | D 65 |

## TURKEY

| | |
|---|---|
| **YUCETEPE** (ex-USS *Orleck*) | D 345 |
| **SAVASTEPE** (ex-USS *Meredith*) | D 348 |
| **KILIÇ ALI PASA** | |
| (ex-USS *Robert H. McCard*) | D 349 |
| **PIYALE PASA** (ex-USS *Fiske*) | D 350 |
| **M. FEVZI ÇAKMAK** | |
| (ex-USS *Charles H. Roan*) | D 351 |
| **GAYRET** (ex-USS *Eversole*) | D 352 |
| **ADATEPE** (ex-USS *Forrest Royal*) | D 353 |
| **KOCATEPE** (ex-USS *Norris*) | D 354 |

**Displacement, tons:** 2 425 standard; 3 500 full load

**Dimensions, feet (metres):** 390.5 × 41.2 × 19 *(119 × 12.6 × 5.8)*

**Aircraft:** 1 Alouette III helicopter *(Themistocles)*

**Guns:** 6—5 in *(127 mm)*/38 (twin Mk 38) (210); 4—5 in *(127 mm)*/38 (twin Mk 38) (remainder); 1—76 mm OTO Melara Compact (aft) (except D 210 and D 215) 1—40 mm (fwd) (212, 213, 214, 215) 4—20 mm Rheinmetal S 20 (single) (amidships in D 210) 2 forward, 2 aft in D 216 and D 217 2—12.7 mm MG (in all)

**Missiles:** SAM; Portable Redeye

**A/S weapons:** 2 fixed Hedgehogs *(Themistocles)*; 1 ASROC 8-barrelled launcher (in remainder); 6 Mk 32 torpedo tubes (2 triple)

**Main engines:** 2 Westinghouse geared turbines; 2 shafts; 60 000 shp

**Boilers:** 4 Babcock & Wilcox

**Speed, knots:** 32.5

**Range, miles:** 4 800 at 15 knots

**Complement:** 269 (16 officers, 253 men)

**Commissioned:** 1944-46 (transferred frrom US Navy 1973-81)

*Themistocles* was a FRAM II Radar Picket conversion, remainder are FRAM I DD conversions.

**Alterations:** The 76 mm Compact is now mounted on the helicopter deck so it is unlikely that helo-operations are possible except in *Themistocles* and *Tompazis*.

**Modernisation:** The Italian Selenia/ELSAG consortium has won the Navy contract for the retrofitting programme of *Krieziz* and *Apostolis*. They will be converted with an Oto-Melara 76/62 mm gun placed aft and a new FCS (NA or NA-21)

## SPAIN

**Commissioned:** 1945 (transferred from US Navy 1972-73). All finally purchased 1978. *Blas de Lezo* has two forward gun mounts and torpedo tubes by after funnel.

## TURKEY

**Commissioned:** 1945-46 (transferred, leased or purchased from US Navy 1971-83). D 349, 353 and 354 FRAM II conversions, remainder FRAM I.

*Gearing class ("Piyale Pasa")*
*10/1984 (L & L van Ginderen)*

| | |
|---|---|
| **HAMBURG** | D 181 |
| **SCHLESWIG-HOLSTEIN** | D 182 |
| **BAYERN** | D 183 |
| **HESSEN** | D 184 |

**Displacement, tons:** 3 340 standard; 4 680 full load

**Dimensions, feet (metres):** 438.5 × 44 × 20.3 *(133.7 × 13.4 × 6.2)*

**Missiles:** SSM; 4 Exocet MM 38 (2 twin launchers)

**Guns:** 3—3.9 in *(100 mm)*/55 (single Mod 1954); 8—40 mm Breda (4 twin)

**A/S weapons:** 2 Bofors 4-barrel 375 mm mortars; 2 DCTs; 4—21 in *(533 mm)* torpedo tubes for A/S torpedoes; DC rails

**Mines:** Can lay mines

**Main engines:** 2 Wahodag geared turbines; 2 shafts; 68 000 shp

**Boilers:** 4 Wahodag; 910 psi *(64 kg/cm²),* 860°F *(460°C)*

**Speed, knots:** 34; 18 economical

**Range, miles:** 6 000 at 13 knots; 920 at 34 knots

**Complement:** 268 (19 officers, 249 men)

**Commissioned:** 1964-68

**Modernisation:** Replacement of 100 mm in X position by four MM 38 Exocet, replacement of 40 mm Bofors by Bredas and addition of two extra A/S torpedo tubes and replacement of LW-02 radar by LW-04.

During later refits bridges have been re-modelled.

Further limited modernisation will be necessary with these ships probably serving until the 1990s.

*Hamburg class ("Hamburg") 7/1982 (Michael D. J. Lennon)*

| | |
|---|---|
| **IMPAVIDO** | D 570 |
| **INTREPIDO** | D 571 |

**Displacement, tons:** 3 201 standard; 3 851 full
   load
**Dimensions, feet (metres):** 429.5 × 44.7 × 14.8
   *(131.3 × 13.6 × 4.5)*
**Missiles:** SAM; Tartar/Standard (est 36; single
   launcher Mk 13)
**Guns:** 2—5 in *(127 mm)*/38 (twin Mk 38) 4—3 in
   *(76 mm)*/62
**A/S weapons:** 2 triple US Mk 32 torpedo tubes
**Main engines:** 2 double reduction geared
   turbines; 2 shafts; 70 000 shp
**Boilers:** 4 Foster-Wheeler; 711 psi *(50 kg/cm²)*;
   842°F *(450°C)*
**Speed, knots:** 33
**Oil fuel, tons:** 650
**Range, miles:** 3 300 at 20 knots; 2 900 at 25
   knots; 1 500 at 30 knots
**Complement:** 340 (23 officers, 317 men)
**Commissioned:** 1963-64

Built under the 1956-57 and 1958-59
programmes respectively. Both ships have
stabilisers.

*Impavido class ('Intrepido') 1985*
*(Milpress)*

| | |
|---|---|
| **KIDD** (ex-*Kouroosh*) | DDG 993 |
| **CALLAGHAN** (ex-*Daryush*) | DDG 994 |
| **SCOTT** (ex-*Nader*) | DDG 995 |
| **CHANDLER** (ex-*Anoushirvan*) | DDG 996 |

**Displacement, tons:** 6 210 light; 8 300 full load
**Dimensions, feet (metres):** 563 × 55 × 30 sonar; 20 keel *(171.6 × 16.8 × 9.1; 6.2)*
**Aircraft:** 2 LAMPS I helicopters (see *Aircraft* notes)
**Missiles:** SSM; 8 Harpoon (2 quad) canister launchers; SAM/ASW; Standard ER (SM-1)/ASROC; (twin Mk 26 launchers)
**Guns:** 2—5 in *(127 mm)*/54 (single Mk 45); 2—20 mm Mk 16 CIWS
**A/S weapons:** 2 triple Mk 32 torpedo tubes; ASROC
**Main engines:** 4 General Electric LM2500 gas turbines; 2 shafts; 80 000 shp
**Speed, knots:** 33
**Range, miles:** 3 300 at 30 knots; 6 000 at 20 knots; 8 000 at 17 knots
**Complement:** 346 (24 officers, 322 enlisted men)
**Commissioned:** 1981-82

Under the approved FY 1979 supplemental budget request the US Navy took over the contracts of four destroyers originally ordered by the Iranian Government in 1974, but cancelled on 3 February 1979 (DDG 995 and 996) and 31 March 1979 (DDG 993 and 994). The four were officially acquired on 25 July 1979. These ships are optimised for general warfare instead of anti-submarine warfare as are the 'Spruance' class. They are the most powerful destroyers in the fleet. Originally, it had been planned to build the entire 'Spruance' class to this design, but because of 'costs' the design was altered to the current plan.

**Aircraft:** To be provided with LAMPS III helicopters.

*Kidd class ("Kidd") 1982 (*Dr. Giorgio Arra*)*

**MUAVENET** (ex-USS *Gwin*)      DM 357

**Displacement, tons:** 2 250 standard; 3 375 full load
**Dimensions, feet (metres):** 376.5 × 40.9 × 19 *(114.8 × 12.5 × 5.8)*
**Guns:** 6—5 in *(127 mm)*/38 (twin Mk 38); 12—40 mm/60 (2 quad Mk 2, 2 twin Mk 1); 11—20 mm/70
**Mines:** 80
**Main engines:** Geared turbines; 2 shafts; 60 000 shp
**Boilers:** 4 Babcock & Wilcox
**Speed, knots:** 34
**Range, miles:** 4 600 at 15 knots
**Complement:** 274
**Commissioned:** 1944

Modified 'Allen M. Sumner' class converted for minelaying. After modernisation at Philadelphia she was transferred on 22 October 1971.

*Robert Smith class ("Muavenet")*
*1978 (*Selcuk Emre*)*

**MARQUÉS DE LA
   ENSENADA**          D 43

**Displacement, tons:** 3 012 standard; 3 785 full
   load
**Dimensions, feet (metres):** 391.5 × 42.7 × 18.4
   *(119.3 × 13 × 5.6)*
**Aircraft:** 1 Hughes 369 HM ASW helicopter
**Guns:** 6—5 in *(127 mm)*/38 (twin Mk 38)
**A/S weapons:** 2 triple Mk 32 tubes for Mk 44
   A/S torpedoes
**Torpedo tubes:** 2—21 in *(533 mm)* fixed single
   Mk 25 tubes for Mk 37 torpedoes
**Main engines:** 2 Rateau-Bretagne geared
   turbines; 2 shafts; 60 000 shp
**Boilers:** Three 3-drum type
**Speed, knots:** 28
**Oil fuel, tons:** 700
**Range, miles:** 4 500 at 15 knots
**Complement:** 318 (20 officers, 298 men)
**Commissioned:** 1970

Ordered in 1948. Towed to Cartagena for
reconstruction to a new design. *Marqués de la
Ensenada* relaunched after being lengthened and
widened on 2 March 1968. Weapons and
electronics identical to 'Gearing (FRAM II)' class.
In autumn 1981 she was damaged in the boiler-
room by a bomb attack by ETA. Repairs to cost
about 10 million pesetas.

*Roger de Lauria class ("Marques de
la Ensenada")*

| | |
|---|---|
| SPRUANCE | DD 963 |
| PAUL F. FOSTER | DD 964 |
| KINKAID | DD 965 |
| HEWITT | DD 966 |
| ELLIOTT | DD 967 |
| ARTHUR W. RADFORD | DD 968 |
| PETERSON | DD 969 |
| CARON | DD 970 |
| DAVID R. RAY | DD 971 |
| OLDENDORF | DD 972 |
| JOHN YOUNG | DD 973 |
| COMTE DE GRASSE | DD 974 |
| O'BRIEN | DD 975 |
| MERRILL | DD 976 |
| BRISCOE | DD 977 |
| STUMP | DD 978 |
| CONOLLY | DD 979 |
| MOOSBRUGGER | DD 980 |
| JOHN HANCOCK | DD 981 |
| NICHOLSON | DD 982 |
| JOHN RODGERS | DD 983 |
| LEFTWICH | DD 984 |
| CUSHING | DD 985 |
| HARRY W. HILL | DD 986 |
| O'BANNON | DD 987 |
| THORN | DD 988 |
| DEYO | DD 989 |
| INGERSOLL | DD 990 |
| FIFE | DD 991 |
| FLETCHER | DD 992 |
| HAYLER | DD 997 |

Above: *Spruance class ("O'Brien")*
*12/1981 (*Dr. Giorgio Arra*)*

Below: *Spruance class ("Hewitt")*
*3/1980 (*Dr. Giorgio Arra*)*

**Displacement, tons:** 5 770 light; 7 810 full load
**Dimensions, feet (metres):** 563.2 × 55.1 × 29
  sonar; 19 keel *(171.7 × 16.8 × 8.8; 5.8)*
**Aircraft:** 1 SH-3 Sea King or 2 SH-2D LAMPS
  helicopters
**Missiles:** SSM; 8 Harpoon (quad) (canisters)
  Tomahawk (ABLs) (see *Missiles* note) SAM;
  one NATO Sea Sparrow; Mk 29 launcher RAM
  (in 1971)
**Guns:** 2—5 in *(127 mm)*/54 (single Mk 45); 2—
  20 mm Mk 16 CIWS Phalanx being fitted
  (already in DD 968-972, 975, 979, 980, 985,
  992, 997)
**A/S weapons:** 1 ASROC 8-tube launcher; 2
  triple torpedo tubes (Mk 32)
**Main engines:** 4 General Electric LM2500 gas
  turbines; 2 shafts; 80 000 shp
**Speed, knots:** 33
**Oil fuel, tons:** 1 400
**Range, miles:** 6 000 at 20 knots
**Complement:** 324 (20 officers, 304 enlisted
  men)
**Commissioned:** 1975-83

DD 997 was added by Congress in FY 1978 as an
air-capable ship, carrying four helicopters. When
the price became too high she was completed as
the thirty-first *Spruance*.

**Missiles:** Tomahawk to be fitted in all ships. In
DD 974, 976, 979, 983, 989 and 990 this has
been or will be fitted in Armoured Box Launchers.
The remainder will be fitted with the Mk 41
Vertical Missile Launch System (VLS) with one
61 missile magazine and replacing the ASROC
launcher.

**Modernisation:** Beginning with FY 1986
overhauls, major improvements will be made to
this class that will enable the 'Spruance' class to
be effective ASW ships into the twenty-first
century.

| SUFFREN | D 602 |
| DUQUESNE | D 603 |

**Displacement, tons:** 5 090 standard; 6 090 full load
**Dimensions, feet (metres):** 517.1 × 50.9 × 20 *(157.6 × 15.5 × 6.1)*
**Missiles:** SSM; 4 Exocet (single launchers); SAM; Masurca (twin launcher)
**Guns:** 2—3.9 in *(100 mm)* (automatic, single); 4—20 mm (single)
**A/S weapons:** Malafon single launcher with 13 missiles; 4 launchers (2 each side) for L5 A/S homing torpedoes
**Main engines:** Double reduction Rateau geared turbines; 2 shafts; 72 500 shp
**Boilers:** 4 automatic; working pressure 640 psi *(45 kg/cm²);* superheat 842°F *(450°C)*
**Speed, knots:** 34
**Range, miles:** 5 100 at 18 knots; 2 400 at 29 knots
**Complement:** 355 (23 officers, 332 men)
**Commissioned:** 1967-70

Ordered under the 1960 programme. Equipped with gyro controlled stabilisers controlling three pairs of non-retractable fins. Air-conditioning of accommodation and operational areas. Excellent sea-boats and weapon platforms.
Both in the Mediterranean.

**Missiles:** Carry 48 Masurca missiles, a mix of Mk 2 Mod 2 beam riders and Mk 2 Mod 3 semi-active homers. During their 1977-78 refit four Exocet launchers replaced the 30 mm gun mountings.

*Suffren class ("Suffren") 5/1982*
*(Michael D. J. Lennon)*

**Batch 1**

| | |
|---|---|
| BIRMINGHAM | D 86 |
| NEWCASTLE | D 87 |
| GLASGOW | D 88 |
| CARDIFF | D 108 |

**Batch 2**

| | |
|---|---|
| EXETER | D 89 |
| SOUTHAMPTON | D 90 |
| NOTTINGHAM | D 91 |
| LIVERPOOL | D 92 |

**Batch 3**

| | |
|---|---|
| MANCHESTER | D 95 |
| GLOUCESTER | D 96 |
| EDINBURGH | D 97 |
| YORK | D 98 |

Left: *Type 42 (Batch 1 "Cardiff")*
*6/1980 (*Michael D. J. Lennon*)*
*Overleaf*
Left: *Type 42 (Batch 2 "Liverpool")*
*10/1985 (*Michael D. J. Lennon*)*
Right: *Type 42 (Batch 3*
*"Manchester") 1984 (*Royal Navy*)*

**Displacement, tons:** 3 500 standard; 4 100 full load (4 775 Batch 3)
**Dimensions, feet (metres):** 392 wl; 412 oa × 47 × 19 (screws) 13.9 (keel) *(119.5; 125 × 14.3 × 5.8; 4.2)*
**Dimensions, feet (metres):** (Batch 3) 434 wl; 462.8 oa × 49 × 19 (screws) *(132.3; 141.1 × 14.9 × 5.8)*
**Aircraft:** 1 Lynx Mk 2 helicopter
**Missiles:** SAM; Sea Dart (1 twin launcher) (surface-to-surface capability)
**Guns:** 1—45 in *(115 mm)*/55 (Mk 8); 2—20mm Oerlikon
**A/S weapons:** Helicopter-launched Mk 44/46 and Stingray torpedoes; 6 A/S torpedo tubes (2 triple) for Mk 46
**Main engines:** COGOG; 2 Rolls-Royce Olympus TM3B gas turbines for full power; 50 000 shp; 2 Rolls-Royce Tyne RM1C gas turbines for cruising; 9 700 shp; cp propellers; 2 shafts
**Speed, knots:** 29 (30+ Batch 3)
**Oil fuel, tons:** 600
**Range:** 4 000 miles at 18 knots
**Complement:** 253 (24 officers, 229 ratings) (accommodation for 312); 301 (26 officers, 275 ratings) (Batch 3)
**Commissioned:** 1976-85

**Class:** In order to provide space for improved weapon systems and to improve speed and seakeeping a radical change was made to this class. From *Manchester* onwards (Batch 3) the beam is increased by 2 ft and the hull length by 42 ft (waterline). *Sheffield* sunk after being struck on 4 May, *Coventry* sunk on 25 May 1982 off the Falkland Islands.

The completion of later ships was somewhat delayed to allow for some modifications resulting from experience in the Falklands' campaign (1982).

| | |
|---|---|
| **DUPETIT THOUARS** | D 625 |
| **DU CHAYLA** | D 630 |

**Displacement, tons:** 2 750 standard; 3 740 full load

**Dimensions, feet (metres):** 421.9 × 41.7 × 21.4 *(128.6 × 12.7 × 6.3)*

**Missiles:** SAM; 40 Tartar SMI or SMIA (single Mk 13 launcher)

**Guns:** 6—57 mm (3 twin)

**A/S weapons:** 2 triple mountings *(550 mm)* for Mk K2 and L3; 1—375 mm Mk 54 projector

**Main engines:** 2 geared turbines; 2 shafts; 63 000 shp

**Boilers:** 4 A & C de B Indret (as in *Duperré*)

**Speed, knots:** 32

**Oil fuel, tons:** 800

**Range, miles:** 5 000 at 18 knots

**Complement:** 277 (17 officers, 260 men) (peace); 320 (war)

**Commissioned:** 1956-57

Originally built as destroyers with six 5 in guns. Converted into DDGs 1961-65.

**Deletions:** *Dupetit Thouars* in 1987 and *Du Chayla* in 1988.

*Type T 47 (DDG) ("Du Chayla")*
*7/1984 (C & S Taylor)*

**LA GALISSONNIÈRE** D 638

**Displacement, tons:** 2 750 standard; 3 910 full load
**Dimensions, feet (metres):** 435.7 × 41.7 × 21.4 *(132.8 × 12.7 × 6.3)*
**Aircraft:** One A/S helicopter
**A/S weapons:** 1 Malafon rocket/homing torpedo launcher
**Guns:** 2—3.9 in *(100 mm)* automatic (single); 1—20 mm
**Torpedo tubes:** 6—21.7 in *(550 mm)* (2 triple for Mks K2 and L3)
**Main engines:** 2 sets Rateau geared turbines; 2 shafts; 63 000 shp
**Boilers:** 4 A & C de B Indret; 500 psi *(35 kg/cm²)*; 617°F *(380°C)*
**Speed, knots:** 34
**Oil fuel, tons:** 800
**Range, miles:** 5 000 at 18 knots
**Complement:** 270 (15 officers, 255 men)
**Commissioned:** 1962

Same characteristics as regards hull and machinery as T 47 and T 53 types, but different armament. She has a hangar which hinges outwards and a platform for landing a helicopter. When first commissioned she was used as an experimental ship for new sonars and anti-submarine weapons.

Began major 8 month refit from September 1983. Recommissioned mid-1984. Due to continue in service until 1990.

*Type T 56 ("La Galissonniere")*
*6/1984 (*L & L van Ginderen*)*

| | |
|---|---|
| D'ESTIENNE D'ORVES*† | F 781 |
| AMYOT D'INVILLE‡ | F 782 |
| DROGOU*† | F 783 |
| DÉTROYAT | F 784 |
| JEAN MOULIN | F 785 |
| QUARTIER MAITRE ANQUETIL*† | F 786 |
| COMMANDANT DE PIMODAN*† | F 787 |
| SECOND MAITRE LE BIHAN‡ | F 788 |
| LIEUTENANT DE VAISSEAU LE HENAFF‡ | F 789 |
| LIEUTENANT DE VAISSEAU LAVALLÉE | F 790 |
| COMMANDANT L'HERMINIER | F 791 |
| PREMIER MAITRE L'HER*† | F 792 |
| COMMANDANT BLAISON* | F 793 |
| ENSEIGNE DE VAISSEAU JACOUBET* | F 794 |
| COMMANDANT DUCUING*† | F 795 |
| COMMANDANT BIROT* | F 796 |
| COMMANDANT BOUAN* | F 797 |

* Exocet fitted
† Mediterranean
‡ Channel
Remainder, Atlantic except *L'Herminier*
(Lorient) and *Blaison* Tahiti.

**Displacement, tons:** 950 standard; 1 170 (1 250 later ships) full load
**Dimensions, feet (metres):** 262.5 × 33.8 × 17.4 (sonar) *(80 × 10.3 × 5.3)*
**Missiles:** SSM; 2 Exocet (single launchers) MM 38 in F781, 783, 786, 787; 4 single launchers MM 40 in 792-797
**Guns:** 1—3.9 in *(100 mm)*; 2—20 mm
**A/S weapons:** 1—375 mm Mk 54 rocket launcher; 4 fixed tubes for Mk L3 and L5 torpedoes
**Main engines:** 2 SEMT-Pielstick 12PC2-V400 (12 PA6 BTC in F 791) diesels; 2 shafts (cp propellers); 12 000 bhp
**Speed, knots:** 24
**Range, miles:** 4 500 at 15 knots
**Endurance, days:** 15
**Complement:** 79 (5 officers, 74 men)
**Commissioned:** 1976-85

Primarily intended for coastal A/S operations—officially classified as 'Avisos'.

**Appearance:** *Jean Moulin* F 785 has a modified funnel, a feature in all ships in due course. All masts are being replaced.

*Type A 69 ("Enseigne de Vaisseau Jacoubet") 9/1985 (*W. Sartori*)*

| | |
|---|---|
| **ALMIRANTE PEREIRA**<br>    **DA SILVA** | F 472 |
| **ALMIRANTE GAGO**<br>    **COUTINHO** | F 473 |
| **ALMIRANTE MAGALHÃES**<br>    **CORREA** | F 474 |

**Displacement, tons:** 1 450 standard; 1 914 full load

**Dimensions, feet (metres):** 314.6 × 36.7 × 17.5 *(95.9 × 11.2 × 5.3)*

**Guns:** 4—3 in *(76 mm)*/50 (twin Mk 33)

**A/S weapons:** 2 Bofors 4-barrelled 375 mm rocket launchers; 6 (2 triple) Mk 32 A/S torpedo tubes

**Main engines:** De Laval dr geared turbines; 1 shaft; 20 000 shp

**Boilers:** 2 Foster-Wheeler, 300 psi, 850°F

**Speed, knots:** 27

**Oil fuel, tons:** 400

**Range, miles:** 3 220 at 15 knots

**Complement:** 168 (14 officers, 154 men)

**Commissioned:** 1966-68

After nearly 20 years' service there are certain maintenance problems with this class. Employed on Coast Guard duties.

**Design:** Similar to the US destroyer escorts of the 'Dealey' class (since deleted), but modified to suit Portuguese requirements.

*Almirante Pereira da Silva class ("Almirante Magalhaes Correa") 7/1980 (*Michael D. J. Lennon*)*

**ALPINO** (ex-*Circe*)      F 580
**CARABINIERE** (ex-*Climene*)      F 581

**Displacement, tons:** 2 700 full load
**Dimensions, feet (metres):** 371.7 × 43.6 × 12.7
    *(113.3 × 13.3 × 3.9)*
**Aircraft:** 2 AB 212 helicopters
**Guns:** 6—3 in *(76 mm)*/62
**A/S weapons:** 1 single semi-automatic DC
    mortar Mk 113; 6 (2 triple) Mk 32 A/S torpedo
    tubes; helicopter torpedoes
**Main engines:** 4 Tosi diesels; 16 800 hp; 2 Tosi
    Metrovick gas turbines; 15 000 hp; 2 shafts
**Speed, knots:** 20 (diesel), 28 (diesel and gas)
**Oil fuel, tons:** 275
**Range, miles:** 3 500 at 18 knots
**Complement:** 163 (13 officers, 150 men)
**Commissioned:** 1968

*Alpino class ("Carabiniere") 7/1985*
*(Dr. Giorgio Arra)*

| | |
|---|---|
| **AMAZON** | F 169 |
| **ACTIVE** | F 171 |
| **AMBUSCADE** | F 172 |
| **ARROW** | F 173 |
| **ALACRITY** | F 174 |
| **AVENGER** | F 185 |

**Displacement, tons:** 2 750 standard; 3 250 full load

**Dimensions, feet (metres):** 360 wl; 384 oa × 41.7 × 19.5 (screws) *(109.7; 117 × 12.7 × 5.9)*

**Aircraft:** 1 Lynx Mk 2 or Wasp helicopter

**Missiles:** SSM; 4 MM 38 Exocet (single cells) SAM; Seacat (1 quad launcher)

**Guns:** 1—4.5 in *(115 mm)*/55 (single Mk 8); 4—20 mm Oerlikon (single)

**A/S weapons:** Helicopter launched torpedoes; 6 (2 triple) torpedo tubes for Mk 46 (see note)

**Main engines:** COGOG; 2 Rolls-Royce Olympus TM3B gas turbines; 50 000 shp; 2 Rolls-Royce Tyne RM1C gas turbines for cruising; 9 700 shp; 2 shafts; cp, 5-bladed propellers

**Speed, knots:** 30; 18 on Tyne GTs

**Range, miles:** 4 000 at 17 knots; 1 200 at 30 knots

**Complement:** 175 (13 officers, and 162 ratings) (accommodation for 192)

**Commissioned:** 1974-78

A contract was awarded to Vosper Thornycroft on 27 February 1968 for the design of a patrol frigate to be prepared in full collaboration with Yarrow Ltd. This is the first custom built gas turbine frigate (designed and constructed as such from the keel up, as opposed to conversion) and the first RN warship designed by commercial firms for many years.

*Ardent* sunk on 21 May, *Antelope* sunk on 23 May 1982 off the Falkland Islands.

*Amazon class ("Arrow") 7/1976*
*(C & S Taylor)*

| | |
|---|---|
| **ANNAPOLIS** | 265 |
| **NIPIGON** | 266 |

**Displacement, tons:** 2 400 standard; 3 000 full load
**Dimensions, feet (metres):** 371 × 42 × 14.4 *(113.1 × 12.8 × 4.4)*
**Aircraft:** 1 CHSS-2 Sea King helicopter
**Guns:** 2—3 in *(76 mm)*/50 US Mk 33 (twin)
**A/S weapons:** 1 Mk 10 Limbo in after well; 6 (2 triple) Mk 32 A/S torpedo tubes
**Main engines:** 2 English Electric geared turbines; 2 shafts; 30 000 shp
**Boilers:** 2 Babcock and Wilcox water tube
**Speed, knots:** 28 (30 on trials)
**Range, miles:** 4 570 at 14 knots
**Complement:** 210 (11 officers, 199 ratings)
**Commissioned:** 1964

These two ships represented the logical development of the original 'St. Laurent' class, through the 'Restigouche' and 'Mackenzie' designs. Due to the erection of a helicopter hangar and flight deck, and variable depth sonar only one Limbo mounting could be installed.

**Modernisation:** A full Delex (Destroyer Life Extension Programme) took place in 1982-84 including Raytheon Seasparrow VLS, new air radar, GFC, communications, sonar and EW equipment. Extension until 1994-96. Cost $24 million per ship.

*Annapolis class ("Annapolis")*
*10/1979 (*Michael D. J. Lennon*)*

| BALEARES | F 71 |
|----------|------|
| ANDALUCIA | F 72 |
| CATALUÑA | F 73 |
| ASTURIAS | F 74 |
| EXTREMADURA | F 75 |

**Displacement, tons:** 3 015 standard; 4 177 full load

**Dimensions, feet (metres):** 438 × 46.9 × 15.4 *(133.6 × 14.3 × 4.7)*

**Missiles:** SSM; 8 Harpoon (F 75); 4 in remainder SAM; 16 Tartar/Standard missiles (lightweight Mk 22 launcher)

**Gun:** 1—5 in *(127 mm)*/L54 (single Mk 42) (see Modernisation note)

**A/S weapons:** 1—8-tube ASROC launcher (8 reloads); 4 Mk 32 for Mk 46 torpedoes; 2 Mk 25 for Mk 37 torpedoes (stern)

**Main engines:** 1 set Westinghouse geared turbines; 1 shaft; 35 000 shp

**Boilers:** 2 high pressure V2M type; 1 200 psi *(84.4 kg/cm²)*

**Speed, knots:** 28

**Range:** 4 500 miles at 20 knots

**Complement:** 256 (15 officers, 241 men)

**Commissioned:** 1973-76

This class resulted from a very close co-operation between Spain and the USA.

**Design:** Generally similar to US Navy's 'Knox' class although they differ in the missile system, hull sonar, Mk 25 torpedo tubes and lack of helicopter facilities.

**Modernisation:** Improvements to bring them to same standard as 'Knox' class. This is due to include fitting of Meroka 20 mm CIWS, Link 11 and NTDS and Mark 1 000 EW system. *Andalucia* begun in 1985.

*Baleares class ("Asturias") 1983*
*(Dr. Giorgio Arra)*

| | |
|---|---|
| **BAPTISTA DE ANDRADE** | F 486 |
| **JOAO ROBY** | F 487 |
| **AFONSO CERQUEIRA** | F 488 |
| **OLIVEIRA E. CARMO** | F 489 |

**Displacement, tons:** 1 250 standard; 1 380 full load
**Dimensions, feet (metres):** 277.5 × 33.8 × 11.8 *(84.6 × 10.3 × 3.6)*
**Guns:** 1—3.9 in *(100 mm)*/55 (single Mod. 1968); 1—40 mm /70 Bofors (single L70)
**A/S weapons:** 2 triple Mk 32 torpedo tubes
**Main engines:** 2 OEW 12-cyl Pielstick diesels; 11 000 bhp = 23.5 knots
**Range, miles:** 5 900 at 18 knots
**Complement:** 122 (11 officers, 111 men), plus marine detachment
**Commissioned:** 1974-75

**Missiles:** Space and weight allowance reserved for two MM 38 Exocet.

*Baptista de Andrade class ("Afonso Cerqueira") 1983 (L & L van Ginderen)*

**VIRGINIO FASAN**                    F 594
**CARLO MARGOTTINI**              F 595

**Displacement, tons:** 1 650 full load
**Dimensions, feet (metres):** 311.7 × 37.4 × 10.5 *(95 × 11.4 × 3.2)*
**Aircraft:** 1 helicopter
**Guns:** 2—3 in *(76 mm)*/62 (single)
**A/S weapons:** 1 single semi-automatic DC mortar Mk 113; 2 triple US Mk 32 for A/S torpedoes
**Main engines:** 4 Fiat diesels; 2 shafts; 16 000 bhp
**Speed, knots:** 24
**Range, miles:** 3 000 at 18 knots
**Complement:** 163 (13 officers, 150 men)
**Commissioned:** 1962

**Modernisation:** A slightly enlarged helicopter platform was fitted and a telescopic hangar shipped to allow for embarkation of one AB 204B helicopter. The after 3 in gun was removed *Carlo Margottini,* 1968; *Virginio Fasan,* 1969. For deletion in 1985.

*Bergamini class ("Carlo Margottini")*
*1980 (*L & L van Ginderen*)*

| | |
|---|---|
| **BERK** | D 358 |
| **PEYK** | D 359 |

**Displacement, tons:** 1 450 standard; 1 950 full load

**Dimensions, feet (metres):** 311.7 × 38.7 × 18.1 *(95 × 11.8 × 5.5)*

**Aircraft:** Helicopter deck

**Guns:** 4—3 in *(76 mm)*/50 (twin)

**A/S weapons:** 6 (2 triple) Mk 32 A/S torpedo tubes; 2 Mk 11 Hedgehogs; 1 DC rack

**Main engines:** 4 Fiat diesels; 2 shafts; 24 000 bhp

**Speed, knots:** 25

**Commissioned:** 1972-75

First major warships built in Turkey, the start of a most important era in the Eastern Mediterranean. Both are named after famous ships of the Ottoman Navy. Of modified US 'Claud Jones' design.

*Berk class ("Peyk") 3/1976 (US Navy)*

| | |
|---|---|
| BREMEN | F 207 |
| NIEDERSACHSEN | F 208 |
| RHEINLAND-PFALZ | F 209 |
| EMDEN | F 210 |
| KÖLN | F 211 |
| KARLSRUHE | F 212 |

**Displacement, tons:** 3 600 full load
**Dimensions, feet (metres):** 426.4 × 47.6 × 21.3
*(130 × 14.5 × 6.5)*
**Aircraft:** 2 Lynx helicopters with AQS 18 sonar
**Missiles:** SSM; 8 Harpoon (2 quad launchers);
SAM; 1—8 cell Sea Sparrow; 2 multiple
Stinger launchers; 2 RAM-ASDM
**Guns:** 1—76 mm/62; Breda 105 mm 20 tube
rocket launcher
**A/S weapons:** 4 Mk 32 torpedo tubes (2 twin)
**Main engines:** 2 GE-LM 2500 gas turbines;
51 600 hp; 2 MTU 20V 956 TB92 diesels;
10 400 hp; 2 shafts; cp propellers
**Speed, knots:** 30-; 20 cruising
**Range, miles:** 4 000 at 18 knots
**Complement:** 204 (of which 6 officers and 12
men are air complement—225 berths
available)
**Commissioned:** 1982-84

Approval given in early 1976 for six of this class,
a modification of the Netherlands 'Kortenaer'
class. Replaced the deleted 'Fletcher', and first
three 'Köln' classes.

**Missiles:** RAM-ASDM not yet fitted in all ships.

*Bremen class ("Rheinland-Pfalz")*

**Batch 1**

| | |
|---|---|
| BROADSWORD | F 88 |
| BATTLEAXE | F 89 |
| BRILLIANT | F 90 |
| BRAZEN | F 91 |

**Batch 2**

| | |
|---|---|
| BOXER | F 92 |
| BEAVER | F 93 |
| BRAVE | F 94 |
| LONDON | F 95 |
| SHEFFIELD | F 96 |
| COVENTRY | F 98 |

**Batch 3**

| | |
|---|---|
| CORNWALL | F 99 |
| CUMBERLAND | F 85 |
| CHATHAM | F 87 |
| CAMPBELTOWN | F 86 |

Left: *Broadsword class (Batch 1 "Battleaxe") 5/1985 (*C & S Taylor*)*
*Overleaf:*
Left: *Broadsword class (Batch 2 "Boxer") 10/1983 (*L & L van Ginderen*)*
Right: *Broadsword class (Batch 3 "Cornwall" artist's impression) (*Yarrow Shipbuilders*)*

**Displacement, tons:** 3 500 standard; 4 400 full load (Batch 1) 4 100 standard; 4 800 full load (Batch 2) 4 200 standard; 4 900 full load (Batch 3)

**Dimensions, feet (metres):** 410 wl; 430 oa × 48.5 × 19.9 (screws) *(125; 131.2 × 14.8 × 6)* (Batch 1)
485.8 oa × 48.5 × 21 (screws) *(148.1 × 14.8 × 6.4)* (Batches 2 and 3)

**Aircraft:** 2 Lynx Mk 2 helicopters with Sea Skua ASM and A/S torpedoes (*Brave* and onwards can operate Sea King or EH 101)

**Missiles:** SSM; 4 Exocet (single cells) (Batches 1 and 2); 8 Harpoon (Batch 3); SAM; Sea Wolf (two 6-barrelled launchers)

**Guns:** (Batch 3) 1—4.5 in *(115 mm)*/55 Mk 8; 1 Goalkeeper; 4—30 mm (twin); (Batches 1 and 2) 2—40 mm/60 (single); 2—20 mm GAM-BO1 (single) (on deployment); 2—20 mm (single)

**A/S weapons:** 6 (2 triple) STWS torpedo tubes for Mk 46; helicopter-carried A/S torpedoes

**Main engines:** COGOG arrangement of 2 Rolls-Royce Olympus TM3B gas turbines; 50 000 shp; 2 Rolls-Royce Tyne RM1C gas turbines; 9 700 shp; 2 shafts; cp propellers (Batch 1, *Boxer, Beaver*) (COGOG arrangement of Rolls-Royce Spey SM1A *(Brave* only*)*) COGAG arrangement of 2 Rolls-Royce Spey SM1A gas turbines; 37 540 shp; 2 Rolls-Royce Tyne RM1C gas turbines; 9 700 shp (remainder of Batch 2 and Batch 3)

**Speed, knots:** 30 (18 on Tynes)
**Range, miles:** 4 500 at 18 knots (on Tynes)
**Complement:** 224 (18 officers, 206 ratings) (accommodation for 248) (Batch 1). 273 (Batches 2 and 3) (accommodation for 296)
**Commissioned:** 1979—89

Originally planned as successors to the 'Leander' class, the construction of which ceased with the completion of the scheduled programme of 26 ships.

This class is primarily designed for A/S operations and is capable of acting as OTC and helicopter control ship.

**BRONSTEIN** FF 1037
**McCLOY** FF 1038

**Displacement, tons:** 2 360 standard; 2 650 full load
**Dimensions, feet (metres):** 371.5 × 40.5 × 23 sonar;
13.5 keel *(113.2 × 12.3 × 7; 4.1)*
**Guns:** 2—3 in *(76 mm)*/50 (twin Mk 33)
**A/S weapons:** 1 ASROC 8-tube launcher; 2 triple torpedo tubes (Mk 32); facilities for small helicopter (no hangar)
**Main engine:** 1 geared turbine (De Laval); 1 shaft; 20 000 shp
**Boilers:** 2 Foster-Wheeler
**Speed, knots:** 26
**Complement:** 305 (16 officers, 289 enlisted men)
**Commissioned:** 1963

These two ships may be considered the first of the 'second generation' of post-Second World War frigates. *Bronstein* and *McCloy* have several features such as hull design, large sonar and ASW weapons that subsequently were incorporated into the mass-produced 'Garcia', 'Brooke', and 'Knox' classes.

Both ships were built under the FY 1960 new construction programme.

*Bronstein class (''Bronstein'')*
*9/1985 (*Dr. Giorgio Arra*)*

| | |
|---|---|
| BROOKE | FFG 1 |
| RAMSEY | FFG 2 |
| SCHOFIELD | FFG 3 |
| TALBOT | FFG 4 |
| RICHARD L. PAGE | FFG 5 |
| JULIUS A. FURER | FFG 6 |

**Displacement, tons:** 2 640 standard; 3 426 full load
**Dimensions, feet (metres):** 414.5 × 44.2 × 24.2 sonar; 15 keel *(126.3 × 13.5 × 7.4; 4.6)*
**Aircraft:** 1 SH-2D LAMPS 1 helicopter
**Missiles:** SAM; Tartar/Standard MR (1 single Mk 22 launcher)
**Gun:** 1—5 in *(127 mm)*/38 (Mk 30)
**A/S weapons:** 1 ASROC 8-tube launcher; 2 triple torpedo tubes (Mk 32)
**Main engines:** 1 geared turbine (Westinghouse in FFG 1- 3, General Electric in others); 1 shaft; 35 000 shp
**Boilers:** 2 Foster-Wheeler
**Speed, knots:** 27.2
**Range, miles:** 4 000 at 20 knots
**Complement:** 332 (20 officers, 312 enlisted men)
**Commissioned:** 1966-67

These ships are identical to the 'Garcia' class frigates except for the Tartar missile system in lieu of a second 5 in gun mount and different electronic equipment.

*Brooke class ("Talbot") 6/1981*
*(Dr. Giorgio Arra)*

**AETOS** (ex-USS *Slater*)  D 01
**IERAX** (ex-USS *Elbert*)  D 31
**LEON** (ex-USS *Eldridge*)  D 54
**PANTHIR** (ex-USS *Garfield
 Thomas*)  D 67

**Displacement, tons:** 1 240 standard; 1 900 full
 load
**Dimensions, feet (metres):** 306 × 36.7 × 14 *(93.3
 × 11.2 × 4.3)*
*Guns:* 3—3 in *(76 mm)*/50 (single Mk 22); 4—
 40 mm/60 (2 twin Mk 1); 14—20 mm/70 (7
 twin)
**Missiles:** SAM; Portable Redeye
**A/S weapons:** 6 Mk 32 torpedo tubes (2 triple);
 Hedgehog; 8 DCTs; 1 DC rack
**Main engines:** 4 sets General Motors diesel-
 electric; 2 shafts; 6 000 bhp
**Speed, knots:** 19.25
**Oil fuel, tons:** 316
**Range, miles:** 9 000 at 12 knots
**Complement:** 220
**Commissioned:** 1943-44

*Aetos* and *Ierax* were transferred on 15 March
1951 and *Leon* and *Panthir* on 15 January 1951.
Their three 21 in torpedo tubes in a triple mount
were removed.

*Cannon class ("Ierax") 7/1980
(Michael D. J. Lennon)*

COMANDANTE JOÃO BELO        F 480
COMANDANTE HERMENEGILDO
    CAPELO                  F 481
COMANDANTE ROBERTO IVENS   F 482
COMANDANTE SACADURA
    CABRAL                  F 483

**Displacement, tons:** 1 750 standard; 2 250 full
    load
**Dimensions, feet (metres):** 340.3 × 38.4 × 15.7
    *(103.7 × 11.7 × 4.8)*
**Guns:** 3—3.9 in *(100 mm)*/55 (single Mod 1953);
    2—40 mm/70
**A/S weapon:** 1—12 in *(305 mm)* quad mortar
**Torpedo tubes:** 6—21 in *(533 mm)* A/S (triple)
**Main engines:** 4 SEMT-Pielstick diesels; 2 shafts;
    16 000 bhp
**Speed, knots:** 25
**Range, miles:** 7 500 at 15 knots
**Complement:** 201 (15 officers, 186 men)
**Commissioned:** 1967-69

**Conversion:** Programme in hand for
modernisation of external communications.

**Design:** They are generally similar to the French
'Commandant Rivière' class except for the 30 mm
guns which were replaced by 40 mm guns.
Designed for tropical service.

*Comandante Joao Belo class*
*("Comandante Joao Belo") 7/1984*
*(L & L van Ginderen)*

| | |
|---|---|
| VICTOR SCHOELCHER | F 725 |
| COMMANDANT BORY | F 726 |
| AMIRAL CHARNER | F 727 |
| DOUDART DE LAGRÉE | F 728 |
| BALNY | F 729 |
| COMMANDANT BOURDAIS | F 740 |
| PROTET | F 748 |
| ENSEIGNE DE VAISSEAU HENRY | F 749 |

**Displacement, tons:** 1 750 standard; 2 250 full load (*Balny* 1 650 standard; 1 950 full load)

**Dimensions, feet (metres):** 340.3 × 38.4 × 15.7 *(103.7 × 11.7 × 4.8)*

**Aircraft:** 1 light helicopter can land aft

**Missiles:** SSM; 4 MM 38 Exocet (single cells) (except *Balny*)

**Guns:** 2—3.9 in *(100 mm)* automatic, single (3 in *Balny*); 2—30 mm

**A/S weapons:** 1—12 in *(305 mm)* quad mortar; 6—21 in *(533 mm)* (2 triple) for Mk K2 and L3

**Main engines:** 4 SEMT-Pielstick diesels; 2 shafts; 16 000 bhp; (except *Balny:* CODAG; 2 diesels (16-cyl); one TG TURBO—MECA M38; 1 shaft; vp screw)

**Speed, knots:** 25

**Range, miles:** 7 500 at 15 knots (*Balny* 8 000 at 12 knots)

**Complement:** 167 (10 officers, 157 men)

**Commissioned:** 1962-70

**Missiles:** All of this class have been fitted with four MM 38 Exocet in place of X gun. *Bory* was the first to be fitted followed by *Doudart de Lagrée*. At the same time the 100 mm gun was replaced in Y position.

**Refit:** *Commandant Rivière* began a major conversion on 26 January 1984 at Lorient. This included a lengthening of the hull to enable new equipment to be fitted for trials purposes and replaced *L'Agenais* on 15 January 1986.

*Commandant Riviere class
("Commandant Bourdais") 2/1985
(L & L van Ginderen)*

| | |
|---|---|
| **DESCUBIERTA** | F 31 |
| **DIANA** | F 32 |
| **INFANTA ELENA** | F 33 |
| **INFANTA CRISTINA** | F 34 |
| **CAZADORA** | F 35 |
| **VENCEDORA** | F 36 |

**Displacement, tons:** 1 233 standard; 1 479 full load

**Dimensions, feet (metres):** 291.3 × 34 × 12.5 *(88.8 × 10.4 × 3.8)*

**Missiles:** SSM; 8 Harpoon (two 4-cell launchers); 1 Octuple Sea Sparrow mounting (16 reloads) (see note)

**Guns:** 1—3 in *(76 mm)*/L62 OTO Melara; 2—40 mm/70 Breda-Bofors (single)

**A/S weapons:** 1—375 mm Bofors twin-barrelled rocket launcher; 6 (2 triple) Mk 32 for Mk 46 torpedoes

**Main engines:** 4 MTU-Bazán 16V 956 TB 91 diesels; 2 shafts; cp propellers; 16 000 bhp (18 000 bhp supercharged for 2 hours)

**Speed, knots:** 25.5

**Range, miles:** 4 000 at 18 knots

**Complement:** 116 (plus 30 Marine detachment)

**Commissioned:** 1978-82

Based on the Portuguese 'Improved João Coutinho' class built by Bazán with modifications to the armament and main engines. Officially rated as corvettes. An improved version (Type 552/A) is under design of 2150 tons full load, 16 m longer and with gas turbines and diesels giving a speed exceeding 30 knots. These ships to be fitted with similar weapons and equipment but with a helicopter and hangar.

**Missiles:** Selenia system (Albatros) for Sea Sparrow. This is built partly in Spain. Harpoon with two 4-cell launchers between bridge and funnel to be fitted.

*Descubierta class ("Cazadora")*
*10/1984 (*L & L van Ginderen*)*

| | |
|---|---|
| GARCIA | FF 1040 |
| BRADLEY | FF 1041 |
| EDWARD McDONNELL | FF 1043 |
| BRUMBY | FF 1044 |
| DAVIDSON | FF 1045 |
| VOGE | FF 1047 |
| SAMPLE | FF 1048 |
| KOELSCH | FF 1049 |
| ALBERT DAVID | FF 1050 |
| O'CALLAHAN | FF 1051 |

**Displacement, tons:** 2 620 standard; 3 403 full load

**Dimensions, feet (metres):** 414.5 × 44.2 × 24 sonar; 14.5 keel *(126.3 × 13.5 × 7.3; 4.4)*

**Aircraft:** 1 SH-2D LAMPS 1 helicopter (except *Sample* and *Albert David*)

**Guns:** 2—5 in *(127 mm)*/38 (single Mk 30)

**A/S weapons:** 1 ASROC 8-tube launcher; 2 triple torpedo tubes (Mk 32)

**Main engines:** 1 geared turbine (Westinghouse in 1040, 1041, 1043-1045; GE in others); 1 shaft; 35 000 shp

**Boilers:** 2 Foster-Wheeler

**Speed, knots:** 27.5

**Complement:** 321 (20 officers, 301 enlisted men)

**Commissioned:** 1964-68

**Torpedoes:** Most of these ships were built with two Mk 25 torpedo tubes built into their transom for launching wire-guided ASW torpedoes. However, they have been removed from the earlier ships and deleted in the later ships. *Voge* and later ships have automatic ASROC reload system (note angled base of bridge structure behind ASROC in these ships).

*Garcia class ("Bradley") 2/1979*
*(Dr. Giorgio Arra)*

**GLOVER**      FF 1098

**Displacement, tons:** 2 643 standard; 3 426 full load

**Dimensions, feet (metres):** 414.5 × 44.2 × 24 sonar *(126.3 × 13.5 × 7.3)*

**Aircraft:** 1 LAMPS 1 helicopter to be installed

**Gun:** 1—5 in *(127 mm)*/38 (Mk 30)

**A/S weapons:** 1 ASROC 8-tube launcher; 2 triple torpedo tubes (Mk 32)

**Main engines:** 1 geared turbine (Westinghouse); 1 shaft; 35 000 shp

**Boilers:** 2 Foster-Wheeler

**Speed, knots:** 27

**Complement:** 328 (17 officers, 311 enlisted men)

**Commissioned:** 1965

The ship was originally authorised in the FY 1960 new construction programme, but was postponed and re-introduced in the FY 1961 programme. Estimated construction cost was $29.33 million.

*Glover* was built to test a new hull design and propulsion system. She was classed as an auxiliary but retained a full combat capability.

**Classification:** *Glover* was originally classified as a miscellaneous auxiliary (AG 163); completed as an escort research ship (AGDE 1). Subsequently changed to frigate research ship (AGFF) on 30 June 1975 and reclassified as a regular frigate on 1 October 1979.

*Glover class ("Glover") 1982*
*(Dr. Giorgio Arra)*

| | |
|---|---|
| **HVIDBJØRNEN** | F 348 |
| **VAEDDEREN** | F 349 |
| **INGOLF** | F 350 |
| **FYLLA** | F 351 |

**Displacement, tons:** 1 345 standard; 1 650 full
load
**Dimensions, feet (metres):** 238.2 × 38 × 16.4
*(72.6 × 11.6 × 5)*
**Aircraft:** 1 Lynx helicopter
**Gun:** 1—3 in *(76 mm)*
**A / S weapons:** DCs
**Main engines:** 4 General Motors 16—567C
diesels; 1 shaft; 6 400 bhp
**Speed, knots:** 18
**Range, miles:** 6 000 at 13 knots
**Complement:** 82
**Commissioned:** 1962-63

Ordered in 1960-61. Of frigate type for fishery
protection and surveying duties in the North Sea,
Faeroe Islands and Greenland waters. They are
equipped with a helicopter platform aft and
hangar.

*Hvidbjornen class ("Ingolf") 1982*
*(Royal Danish Navy)*

**BESKYTTEREN** F 340

**Displacement, tons:** 1 970 full load
**Dimensions, feet (metres):** 245 × 40 × 17.4 *(74.7 × 12.2 × 5.3)*
**Aircraft:** 1 Lynx helicopter
**Gun:** 1—3 in *(76 mm)*
**Main engines:** 3 Burmeister & Wain Alpha diesels; 1 shaft; 7 440 bhp
**Speed, knots:** 18
**Range, miles:** 4 500 at 16 knots on 2 engines; 6 000 at 13 knots on 1 engine
**Complement:** 67
**Commissioned:** 1976

Cost approximately £5 million. Strengthened for navigation in ice. Designed for similar duties as *Hvidbjørnen.*

*Modified Hvidbjornen class ("Beskytteren") (*Michael D. J. Lennon*)*

| JACOB VAN HEEMSKERCK | F 812 |
| WITTE DE WITH | F 813 |

**Displacement, tons:** 3 750 full load approx
**Dimensions, feet (metres):** 428 × 47.9 × 14.1
*(130.5 × 14.6 × 4.3)*
**Missiles:** SSM; 8 Harpoon SAM; SM-1 (MR), Mk
13 launcher; NATO Sea Sparrow PDMS
**Gun:** 1 Goalkeeper VSR/ADS
**A/S weapons:** 4 Mk 32 torpedo tubes (twin)
**Main engines:** 2 Rolls-Royce Olympus TM3B gas
turbines = 50 000 shp; 2 Rolls-Royce Tyne
RM1C gas turbines = 8 000 shp; 2 cp propellers
**Speed, knots:** 30
**Range, miles:** 4 700 on Tyne cruising turbines at
16 knots
**Complement:** 200
**Commissioned:** 1986

Ordered as replacement construction for the two
'Kortenaer' class frigates sold to Greece. Air
defence frigates with command facilities for a
task group commander and his staff. *Witte de
With* started trials mid-1986.

*Jacob van Heemskerck class ("Jacob
van Heemskerck") (*L & L van
Ginderen*)*

| | |
|---|---|
| **ANTONIO ENES** | F 471 |
| **JOÃO COUTINHO** | F 475 |
| **JACINTO CANDIDO** | F 476 |
| **GENERAL PEREIRA D'EÇA** | F 477 |
| **AUGUSTO DE CASTILHO** | F 484 |
| **HONORIO BARRETO** | F 485 |

**Displacement, tons:** 1 203 standard; 1 380 full load
**Dimensions, feet (metres):** 277.5 × 33.8 × 11.8 *(84.6 × 10.3 × 3.6)*
**Guns:** 2—3 in *(76 mm)*/50 (twin Mk 34); 2—40 mm/70
**Main engines:** 2 OEW 12-cyl Pielstick diesels; 10 560 bhp
**Speed, knots:** 24.4
**Range, miles:** 5 900 at 18 knots
**Complement:** 100 (9 officers, 91 men) plus marine detachment of 34
**Commissioned:** 1970-71

**Modernisation:** A programme for this class is planned.

*Joao Coutinho class ("Antonio Enes") 1983 (*L & L van Ginderen*)*

| | | | | |
|---|---|---|---|---|
| KNOX | FF 1052 | AYLWIN | FF 1081 |
| ROARK | FF 1053 | ELMER MONTGOMERY | FF 1082 |
| GRAY | FF 1054 | COOK | FF 1083 |
| HEPBURN | FF 1055 | McCANDLESS | FF 1084 |
| CONNOLE | FF 1056 | DONALD B. BEARY | FF 1085 |
| RATHBURNE | FF 1057 | BREWTON | FF 1086 |
| MEYERKORD | FF 1058 | KIRK | FF 1087 |
| W. S. SIMS | FF 1059 | BARBEY | FF 1088 |
| LANG | FF 1060 | JESSE L. BROWN | FF 1089 |
| PATTERSON | FF 1061 | AINSWORTH | FF 1090 |
| WHIPPLE | FF 1062 | MILLER | FF 1091 |
| REASONER | FF 1063 | THOMAS C. HART | FF 1092 |
| LOCKWOOD | FF 1064 | CAPODANNO | FF 1093 |
| STEIN | FF 1065 | PHARRIS | FF 1094 |
| MARVIN SHIELDS | FF 1066 | TRUETT | FF 1095 |
| FRANCIS HAMMOND | FF 1067 | VALDEZ | FF 1096 |
| VREELAND | FF 1068 | MOINESTER | FF 1097 |
| BAGLEY | FF 1069 | | |
| DOWNES | FF 1070 | | |
| BADGER | FF 1071 | | |
| BLAKELY | FF 1072 | | |
| ROBERT E. PEARY | FF 1073 | | |
| HAROLD E. HOLT | FF 1074 | | |
| TRIPPE | FF 1075 | | |
| FANNING | FF 1076 | | |
| OUELLET | FF 1077 | | |
| JOSEPH HEWES | FF 1078 | | |
| BOWEN | FF 1079 | | |
| PAUL | FF 1080 | | |

Left: *Knox class ("Francis Hammond")*
*8/1980 (Dr. Giorgio Arra)*
*Overleaf:*
Left: *Knox class ("McCandless")*
*1/1986 (Dr. Giorgio Arra)*
Right: *Knox class ("McCandless")*
*(Dr. Giorgio Arra)*

**Displacement, tons:** 3 011 standard; 3 877 (1052-1077) 4 200 (remainder) full load (see *Modification* note)
**Dimensions, feet (metres):** 438 × 46.8 × 24.8 sonar; 15 keel *(133.5 × 14.3 × 7.8; 4.6)*
**Aircraft:** 1 SH-2 LAMPS helicopter
**Missiles:** SSM; 8 Harpoon; 4 Tomahawk (see *Missiles* note) SAM; 1 Sea Sparrow BPDMS multiple launcher (Mk 25) in some being replaced by Phalanx
**Guns:** 1—5 in *(127 mm)*/54 (Mk 42); 1—20 mm Phalanx Mk 16 (to replace Sea Sparrow in all)
**A/S weapons:** 1 ASROC 8-tube launcher; 4 fixed torpedo tubes (Mk 32)
**Main engines:** 1 geared turbine (Westinghouse); 1 shaft; 35 000 shp

**Boilers:** 2 Combustion Engineering (except FF 1056, 1057, 1061, 1063, 1065, 1072, 1073, 1075, 1077 which have Babcock & Wilcox)
**Speed, knots:** 27
**Complement:** 329 (19 officers, 310 enlisted men)
**Commissioned:** 1969-74

**Modifications:** In 1979 a programme was initiated to fit 3.5 ft bow bulwarks and spray strakes to all ships of the class adding 9.1 tons to the displacement. This is being fitted to all ships at their next overhaul.

## GERMANY, FR

| | |
|---|---|
| **AUGSBURG** | F 222 |
| **LÜBECK** | F 224 |

## TURKEY

| | |
|---|---|
| **GELIBOLU** (ex-*Karlsruhe*) | D 360 |
| **GEMLIK** (ex-*Emden*) | D 361 |

**Displacement, tons:** 2 100 standard; 2 700 full load

**Dimensions, feet (metres):** 360.5 × 36.1 × 16.7 (sonar) *(109.9 × 11 × 5.1)*

**Guns:** 2—3.9 in *(100 mm)*/55 (single mod 1954) 6—40 mm (2 twin and 2 single)

**A/S weapons:** 2 Bofors 4-barrel DC mortars (72 charges); 4—21 in *(533 mm)* (single) for A/S torpedoes; 2 DCTs; DC rails.

**Mines:** Can carry 80

**Main engines:** Combined diesel and gas turbine plant; 4 MAN 16-cyl diesels; total 12 000 bhp; 2 Brown Boveri gas turbines, 24 000 bhp; total 36 000 bhp; 2 shafts

**Speed, knots:** 28; 18 economical

**Oil fuel, tons:** 333

**Range, miles:** 920 at 28 knots

**Complement:** 210 (17 officers, 193 men)

**Commissioned:** 1962-64

## TURKEY

**Transfers:** Both transferred by Federal German Navy. D 360 commissioned 28 March 1983; D 361, 23 September 1983.

*Köln class ("Augsburg") 5/1985 (L & L van Ginderen)*

## NETHERLANDS

| | |
|---|---|
| **KORTENAER** | F 807 |
| **CALLENBURGH** | F 808 |
| **VAN KINSBERGEN** | F 809 |
| **BANCKERT** | F 810 |
| **PIET HEYN** | F 811 |
| **ABRAHAM CRIJNSSEN** | F 816 |
| **PHILIPS VAN ALMONDE** | F 823 |
| **BLOYS VAN TRESLONG** | F 824 |
| **JAN VAN BRAKEL** | F 825 |
| **PIETER FLORISZ** | |
| (ex-*Willem van der Zaan*) | F 826 |

## GREECE

| | |
|---|---|
| **ELLI** (ex-*Pieter Florisz*) | F 450 |
| **LIMNOS** (ex-*Witte de With*) | F 451 |

**Displacement, tons:** 3 050 standard; 3 630 full load

**Dimensions, feet (metres):** 428 × 47.9 × 20.3 (screws); 14.1 *(130.5 × 14.6 × 6.2; 4.3)*

**Aircraft:** 2 Lynx helicopters

**Missiles:** SSM; 8 Harpoon SAM; NATO Sea Sparrow PDMS

**Guns:** 1—76 mm/62 (Compact); 1—40 mm (see notes)

**A/S weapons:** 4 (2 twin) Mk 32 torpedo tubes for Mk 46 torpedoes in after deckhouse

**Main engines:** 2 Rolls-Royce Olympus TM3B gas turbines = 50 000 shp; 2 Rolls-Royce Tyne RM1C gas turbines = 8 000 shp; 2 vp propellers

**Speed, knots:** 30

**Range, miles:** 4 700 on Tyne cruising turbines at 16 knots

**Complement:** 176 (including air personnel).

**Commissioned:** 1978-83

**Gunnery:** VSR ADS Type Signaal Goalkeeper is to be mounted on top of hangar. 40 mm mounted in lieu except in *Pieter Florisz* (with an extra 76 mm) until Goalkeeper is available. Two systems were completed in 1982 for trials. One was mounted in *Callenburgh* autumn 1983 for final sea trials. Ten more ordered in 1983—to be fitted as available.

## GREECE

A contract was signed with the Netherlands on 15 September 1980 for the purchase of one of the 'Kortenaer' class currently building for the Netherlands' Navy, delivery to be in late 1981 and an option on second of class, which was taken up 7 June 1981. At the same time it was announced that a third of the class would be built in Greece at the Hellenic Shipyards, Skaramanga with at least two more to follow. The local building programme, however, appears to be in abeyance.

*Kortenaer class ("Piet Heyn") 1985*
*(J. A. Verhoog)*

**IKARA GROUP (Batch 1)**

| | |
|---|---|
| AURORA | F 10 |
| EURYALUS | F 15 |
| GALATEA | F 18 |
| ARETHUSA | F 38 |
| NAIAD | F 39 |
| LEANDER | F 109 |

**EXOCET GROUP (Batch 2 T.A.)**

| | |
|---|---|
| CLEOPATRA | F 28 |
| SIRIUS | F 40 |
| PHOEBE | F 42 |
| ARGONAUT | F 56 |

**EXOCET GROUP (Batch 2)**

| | |
|---|---|
| MINERVA | F 45 |
| DANAE | F 47 |
| JUNO (see *Training* note) | F 52 |
| PENELOPE | F 127 |

**BROAD-BEAMED GROUP**
**(Batch 3 Conversions)**

| | |
|---|---|
| ANDROMEDA | F 57 |
| HERMIONE | F 58 |
| JUPITER | F 60 |
| SCYLLA | F 71 |
| CHARYBDIS | F 75 |

**BROAD-BEAMED GROUP**
**(Batch 3)**

| | |
|---|---|
| ACHILLES | F 12 |
| DIOMEDE | F 16 |
| APOLLO | F 70 |
| ARIADNE | F 72 |

*Leander class (Batch 3 "Charybdis")*
*8/1982 (*Michael D. J. Lennon*)*

**Displacement, tons:** 2 450 standard; 2 860 full load (Ikara group); 3 200 full load (Exocet groups); 2 500 standard; 2 962 full load (Broad-beamed group)

**Dimensions, feet (metres):** 360 wl; 372 oa × 41 × 14.8 (keel); 18 (screws) *(109.7; 113.4 × 12.5 × 4.5; 5.5)* Broad-beamed groups (beam) 43 ft *(13.1 m)*; Exocet group draught (screws) 19 ft *(5.8 m)*

**Aircraft:** 1 Lynx Mk 2 or Wasp helicopter (except *Cleopatra*)

**Missiles:** Batch 1: ASW; Ikara SAM; 2 quad Seacat.
Batch 2: (T.A.): SSM; 4 MM 38 Exocet SAM; 2 quad Seacat.
Batch 2: SSM; 4 MM 38 Exocet SAM; 3 quad Seacat. Batch 3 (Conversions): SSM; 4 MM 38 Exocet SAM; 1 Sea Wolf.
Batch 3: SAM; 1 quad Seacat

**Guns:** Batch 1: 2—40 mm/60
Batch 2 (T.A.): 2—20 mm (single)
Batch 2: 2—40 mm/60 (2—20 mm single in *Juno*)
Batch 3 (Conversions): 2—20 mm
Batch 3: 2—4.5 in *(115 mm)*/45 (twin Mk 6); 2—20 mm/70 (plus 1 additional 20 mm single GAM-BO1 on after end of flight deck)

**A/S weapons:** Ikara group: Ikara (fwd)(GWS 40); 1 Limbo (aft)
Exocet group: 2 triple STWS torpedo tubes
Broad-beamed groups: 1—3-barrelled A/S mortar Mk 10 (unconverted); 2 triple STWS torpedo tubes (conversions)

**Main engines:** 2 double reduction geared turbines; 2 shafts; 30 000 shp

**Boilers:** 2

**Speed, knots:** 28

**Oil fuel, tons:** 460

**Range, miles:** 4 000 at 15 knots

**Complement:** 257 (19 officers, 238 ratings) (Ikara group); 248 (20 officers, 228 ratings) (Exocet group); 260 (19 officers, 241 ratings) (Broad-beamed conversions); 235 (15 officers, 220 ratings) (Broad-beamed groups)

**Commissioned:** 1972-85

**Conversions:** Batch 3 conversion includes the provision of four MM 38 Exocet launchers, the Sea Wolf SAM system, improved sonar, Lynx helicopter, modern EW equipment and STWS torpedo tubes. At the same time the 4.5 in turret, Seacat and Limbo are removed.

A further conversion of four of Batch 2 (listed above as Batch 2 T.A.) and *Arethusa* has included the installation of a towed array on the quarter-deck. As a result of this extra 70 tons of top-weight the forward Seacat has been removed, the bridge 40 mm guns replaced by 20 mms, the Exocet mountings have been lowered, boats have been replaced by a Pacific 22 craft and small crane, the Type 965 radar aerial removed and the STWS torpedo tubes moved down a deck.

Above: *Leander class (Batch 1
"Arethusa") 7/1984 (*L & L van
Ginderen*)*

Right: *Leander class (Batch 2
"Cleopatra") 1977 (*Royal Navy*)*

| | |
|---|---|
| **LUPO** | F 564 |
| **SAGITTARIO** | F 565 |
| **PERSEO** | F 566 |
| **ORSA** | F 567 |

**Displacement, tons:** 2 208 standard; 2 500 full load

**Dimensions, feet (metres):** 371.3 × 37.1 × 12.1 *(113.2 × 11.3 × 3.7)*

**Aircraft:** AB 212 helicopter (see *Aircraft* note)

**Missiles:** SSM; 8 Teseo launchers SAM; NATO Sea Sparrow (8 cell launcher) (see *Missile* note)

**Guns:** 1—5 in *(127 mm)*/54 (Compact) 4—40 mm/70 (twin Breda Compact) (twin Dardo systems)

**A/S weapons:** 6 (2 triple) US Mk 32 torpedo tubes; helicopter torpedoes

**Main engines:** CODOG—2 Fiat LM 2500 gas turbines; 50 000 hp; 2 GMT A230.20M diesels; 7 800 hp; 2 shafts (cp propellers)

**Speed, knots:** 35 on turbines; 21 on diesels

**Range, miles:** 4 350 at 16 knots (diesels)

**Complement:** 185 (16 officers, 169 ratings)

**Commissioned:** 1977-80

*Lupo class ("Perseo") 7/1981*
*(Dr. Giorgio Arra)*

The decision to build the 'Maestrale' Class which is 34 ft longer and 5 ft wider in the beam was prompted by the need for a fleet ASW ship whereas 'Lupo' class was designed primarily for convoy escort work with a surface warfare capability.

**Aircraft:** Telescopic hangar for helicopter.

**Missiles:** NATO Sea Sparrow modified to fire Aspide missiles in addition.

| MACKENZIE | 261 |
| SASKATCHEWAN | 262 |
| YUKON | 263 |
| QU'APPELLE | 264 |

**Displacement, tons:** 2 380 standard; 2 880 full load
**Dimensions, feet (metres):** 366 × 42 × 13.5 *(111.6 × 12.8 × 4.1)*
**Guns:** 4—3 in *(76 mm)* (1 twin Mk 6 fwd, 1 twin Mk 33 aft); *(Qu'Appelle;* 2—3 in *(76 mm)*/50 (twin Mk 33))
**A/S weapons:** 2 Mk 10 Limbo in well aft; 6 (2 triple) Mk 32 A/S torpedo tubes
**Main engines:** 2 English Electric geared turbines; 2 shafts; 30 000 shp
**Boilers:** 2 Babcock and Wilcox water tube
**Speed, knots:** 28
**Range, miles:** 4 750 at 14 knots
**Complement:** 210 (11 officers, 199 ratings)
**Commissioned:** 1962-63

**Modernisation:** All being modernised at Esquimalt by Burrard/Yarrow Inc under Delex (Destroyer Life Extension Programme) 1982-85 including new sonar and communications, and modifications to SP 12 radar. Extension until 1990-93. Cost $12 million per ship.

*Mackenzie class ("Mackenzie")*
*10/1982 (*L & L van Ginderen*)*

| | |
|---|---|
| MAESTRALE | F 570 |
| GRECALE | F 571 |
| LIBECCIO | F 572 |
| SCIROCCO | F 573 |
| ALISEO | F 574 |
| EURO | F 575 |
| ESPERO | F 576 |
| ZEFFIRO | F 577 |

**Displacement, tons:** 2 500 standard; 3 040 full load

**Dimensions, feet (metres):** 405 × 42.5 × 27.4 (screws) *(122.7 × 12.9 × 8.4)*

**Aircraft:** 2 AB 212 helicopters

**Missiles:** SSM; 4 Teseo launchers SAM; Albatros with Aspide missiles (8 cell launcher)

**Guns:** 1—5 in *(127 mm)*/54 (Compact) 4—40 mm/70 (Breda Compact—twin)

**A/S weapons:** 2 triple US Mk 32 torpedo tubes; helicopter torpedoes

**Torpedo tubes:** 2 for A 184 torpedoes in transom

**Main engines:** CODOG; 2 Fiat LM 2500 gas turbines; 50 000 shp; 2 GMT B 230.50 DVM diesels; 11 000 hp; 2 shafts (cp propellers)

**Speed, knots:** 32 (gas); 21 (diesels)

**Range, miles:** 6 000 at 16 knots

**Complement:** 232 (24 officers, 208 ratings)

**Commissioned:** 1982—84

There has been a notable increase of 34 ft in length and 5 ft in beam over the 'Lupo' class to provide for the fixed hangar and VDS, the result providing more comfortable accommodation. First six ordered December 1976 and last pair in October 1980. Fitted with stabilisers. Good A/S capability and an integrated gun/missile control system.

*Maestrale class ("Espero") 7/1985*
*(Dr. Giorgio Arra)*

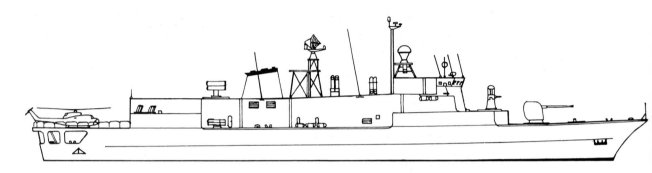

**YAVUZ**                                    F 240

**Number in class: 4**

**Displacement, tons:** 2 000 standard; 2 784 full
   load
**Dimensions, feet (metres):** 362.4 × 46.6 × 13.1
   *(110.5 × 13.3 × 4)*
**Aircraft:** Deck and hangar for 1 AB 212
   helicopter
**Missiles:** SSM; 8 Harpoon (quad) SAM; Sea
   Sparrow with Aspide missiles
**Guns:** 1—5 in *(127 mm)* US Mk 45; 3 Seaguard
   CIWS with Oerlikon Zenith 4-barrelled 25 mm
**A/S weapons:** 6 (2 triple) Mk 32 ASW torpedo
   tubes
**Main engines:** 4 MTU 20V 1163 TB93 diesels; 2
   shafts (cp propellers); 20 400 hp
**Speed, knots:** 28
**Range, miles:** 4 000 at 20 knots
**Complement:** 180
**Commissioned:** due 1987 (plus 3 others on order
   or building)

Full order signed 7 September 1983 with builders
and Thyssen Rheinstahl Technik of Düsseldorf.
Fabrication of first ship started September 1983.

*'MEKO 200' type*

**NIELS JUEL**     F 354
**OLFERT FISCHER**     F 355
**PETER TORDENSKIOLD**     F 356

**Displacement, tons:** 1 320 full load
**Dimensions, feet (metres):** 275.5 × 33.8 × 10.2
   *(84 × 10.3 × 3.1)*
**Missiles:** SSM; 8 Harpoon (two 4-cell launchers)
   SAM; 8 Sea Sparrow (8-cell launcher)
**Gun:** 1—76 mm/62 OTO Melara Compact
**A/S weapons:** 4 Mk 32 torpedo tubes (built into
   hull)
**Mines:** Have laying capability
**Rocket projectors:** 2 for illumination, chaff and
   Sea Gnat HE rockets
**Main engines:** CODOG; General-Electric LM
   2500 gas turbine; 18 400 shp; 1 MTU 20 V 956
   TB82 diesel; max 4 500 hp; SSS clutches; GEC
   gearbox; 2 shafts
**Speed, knots:** 30 (gas-max 26 000 shp) (28 gas
   at 18 400 shp); 20 on diesel
**Range, miles:** 2 500 at 18 knots
**Complement:** 98
**Commissioned:** 1980-82

Y-ARD Glasgow designed the class to Danish
order. On 5 December 1975 announced that they
would be built by Aalborg Vaerft.

*Niels Juel class ("Niels Juel")*
*4/1985 (*Maritime Photographic*)*

# USA

| | |
|---|---|
| OLIVER HAZARD PERRY | FFG 7 |
| McINERNEY | FFG 8 |
| WADSWORTH | FFG 9 |
| DUNCAN | FFG 10 |
| CLARK | FFG 11 |
| GEORGE PHILIP | FFG 12 |
| SAMUEL ELIOT MORISON | FFG 13 |
| JOHN H. SIDES | FFG 14 |
| ESTOCIN | FFG 15 |
| CLIFTON SPRAGUE | FFG 16 |
| JOHN A. MOORE | FFG 19 |
| ANTRIM | FFG 20 |
| FLATLEY | FFG 21 |
| FAHRION | FFG 22 |
| LEWIS B. PULLER | FFG 23 |
| JACK WILLIAMS | FFG 24 |
| COPELAND | FFG 25 |
| GALLERY | FFG 26 |
| MAHLON S. TISDALE | FFG 27 |
| BOONE | FFG 28 |
| STEPHEN W. GROVES | FFG 29 |
| REID | FFG 30 |
| STARK | FFG 31 |
| JOHN L. HALL | FFG 32 |
| JARRETT | FFG 33 |
| AUBREY FITCH | FFG 34 |
| UNDERWOOD | FFG 36 |
| CROMMELIN | FFG 37 |
| CURTS | FFG 38 |
| DOYLE | FFG 39 |
| HALYBURTON | FFG 40 |
| McCLUSKY | FFG 41 |
| KLAKRING | FFG 42 |
| THACH | FFG 43 |

*Oliver Hazard Perry class ("Mahlon S Tisdale") 10/1985 (Dr. Giorgio Arra)*

| | |
|---|---|
| De WERT | FFG 45 |
| RENTZ | FFG 46 |
| NICHOLAS | FFG 47 |
| VANDEGRIFT | FFG 48 |
| ROBERT G. BRADLEY | FFG 49 |
| TAYLOR | FFG 50 |
| GARY | FFG 51 |
| CARR | FFG 52 |
| HAWES | FFG 53 |
| FORD | FFG 54 |
| ELROD | FFG 55 |
| SIMPSON | FFG 56 |
| REUBEN JAMES | FFG 57 |
| SAMUEL B. ROBERTS | FFG 58 |
| KAUFFMAN | FFG 59 |
| RODNEY M. DAVIS | FFG 60 |
| INGRAHAM | FFG 61 |

**Displacement, tons:** 2 750 light; 3 585 full load
**Dimensions, feet (metres):** 445 × 45 × 24.5 sonar; 14.8 keel *(135.6 × 13.7 × 7.5; 4.5)* (FFG 8, 36-43, 45-61 length 453 *(138.1)*)
**Aircraft:** 2 SH-2 LAMPS helicopters
**Missiles:** SSM/SAM; Harpoon/Standard (1 single Mk 13 launcher)
**Guns:** 1—76 mm/62 (Mk 75); 1—20 mm CIWS Mk 16 Phalanx
**A/S weapons:** 2 triple torpedo tubes (Mk 32)
**Main engines:** 2 LM 2500 gas turbines (General Electric); 1 shaft (cp propeller); 40 000 shp
**Speed, knots:** 29
**Range, miles:** 4 500 at 20 knots
**Complement:** 200 (12 officers, 188 enlisted men) (includes 19 aircrew)
**Commissioned:** 1977-88

# SPAIN ('FFG 7' CLASS)

| | |
|---|---|
| SANTA MARIA | F 81 |
| VICTORIA | F 82 |
| NUMANCIA | F 83 |

The Spanish-built 'FFG 7' class differ in having a displacement of 3605 tons full load, 1-Meroka gun system instead of 20mm CIWS Mk 16 Phalanx, a speed of 30 knots and a complement of 204 (14 officers and 190 ratings, including aircrew).

**Commissioned:** 1986-88 (plus one on order)

| | |
|---|---|
| **OSLO** | F 300 |
| **BERGEN** | F 301 |
| **TRONDHEIM** | F 302 |
| **STAVANGER** | F 303 |
| **NARVIK** | F 304 |

**Displacement, tons:** 1 450 standard; 1 745 full load

**Dimensions, feet (metres):** 317 × 36.8 × 18 (screws) *(96.6 × 11.2 × 5.5)*

**Missiles:** SSM; 6 Penguin SAM; Octuple Sea Sparrow

**Guns:** 4—3 in *(76 mm)* (2 twin mounts US Mk 33)

**A/S weapons:** 6 (2 triple) Mk 32 torpedo tubes; Terne III system with 6-barrelled rocket launcher

**Mines:** Laying capability

**Main engines:** 1 set De Laval Ljungstrom double reduction geared turbines; 1 shaft; 20 000 shp

**Boilers:** 2 Babcock & Wilcox

**Speed, knots:** 25+

**Complement:** 150 (11 officers, 139 ratings)

**Commissioned:** 1966-67

The hull and propulsion design of these ships is based on that of the 'Dealey' class destroyer escorts of the US Navy, but considerably modified to suit Norwegian requirements.

**Modernisation:** All ships to be modernised with improvements in radar and electronics with Spherion TSM-2633 sonar (a joint Thomson CSF/Simrad-Subsea (Norway) project to be provided by Simrad). The after 76 mm mounting may be replaced by an unspecified CIWS. The class will serve into the 1990s to be relieved by new construction.

*Oslo class ("Stavanger") 3/1985*
*(L & L van Ginderen)*

| | |
|---|---|
| **PEDER SKRAM** | F 352 |
| **HERLUF TROLLE** | F 353 |

**Displacement, tons:** 2 030 standard; 2 720 full load

**Dimensions, feet (metres):** 396.5 × 39.5 × 11.8 *(112.6 × 12 × 3.6)*

**Missiles:** SSM; 8 Harpoon (two 4-cell launchers) SAM; Sea Sparrow (one 4-cell launcher with 16 missiles)

**Guns:** 2—5 in *(127 mm)*/38 (twin Mk 38); 4—40 mm/60

**Torpedo tubes:** 4—21 in *(533 mm)* for wire-guided and A/S torpedoes

**A/S weapons:** DCs

**Main engines:** CODOG; 2 General Motors 16-567 D diesels; 4 800 hp; 2 Pratt & Whitney PWA GG 4A-3 gas turbines; 44 000 hp total output; 2 shafts

**Speed, knots:** 32.5 gas; 16.5 diesel

**Complement:** 191

**Commissioned:** 1966-67

Danish design. In addition to other armament they were originally designed for three 21 in torpedo tubes and the Terne anti-submarine weapon, but the latter has been dropped in favour of Sea Sparrow and two twin 21 in mountings fitted on the beams.

To be paid off to ready reserve with maintenance crew in 1987.

**Conversion:** Mid-life conversion in 1977-78,

*Peder Skram class ("Peder Skram")*
*(*Royal Danish Navy*)*

| | |
|---|---|
| **CHAUDIERE** | 235 |
| **ST. CROIX** | 256 |
| **COLUMBIA** | 260 |

**Displacement, tons:** 2 370 standard; 2 880 full load

**Dimensions, feet (metres):** 366 × 42 × 13.5 *(111.6 × 12.8 × 4.1)*

**Guns:** 4—3 in *(76 mm)*/70 (twin Mk 6 fwd, twin Mk 33 aft)

**A/S weapons:** 2 Mk 10 Limbo in well aft; side launchers for Mk 43 torpedoes

**Main engines:** Geared turbines; 2 shafts; 30 000 shp

**Boilers:** 2 water tube

**Speed, knots:** 28

**Range, miles:** 4 750 at 14 knots

**Complement:** 248 (12 officers, 236 ratings)

**Commissioned:** 1958-59

All three paid off into Category C Reserve in 1974.

*St. Croix* now in Training Reserve alongside in Halifax.

*Restigouche class ("Columbia")*
*(*Michael D. J. Lennon*)*

| | |
|---|---|
| **GATINEAU** | 236 |
| **RESTIGOUCHE** | 257 |
| **KOOTENAY** | 258 |
| **TERRA NOVA** | 259 |

**Displacement, tons:** 2 390 standard; 2 900 full load

**Dimensions, feet (metres):** 371 × 42 × 14.1 *(113.1 × 12.8 × 4.3)*

**Guns:** 2—3 in *(76 mm)*/70 (twin Mk 6)

**A/S weapons:** ASROC aft and 1 Mk 10 Limbo in after well

**Main engines:** 2 English Electric geared turbines; 2 shafts; 30 000 shp

**Boilers:** 2 Babcock and Wilcox water tube

**Speed, knots:** 28

**Range, miles:** 4 750 at 14 knots

**Complement:** 214 (13 officers, 201 ratings)

**Commissioned:** 1959

**Conversion:** These four ships were refitted with ASROC aft and lattice foremast. Work included removing the after 3 in/50 twin gun mounting and one Limbo A/S Mk 10 triple mortar, to make way for ASROC and variable depth sonar. *Terra Nova*'s refit was completed on 18 October 1968: *Gatineau* completed in 1972 and *Kootenay* and *Restigouche* in 1973. Refit also included improvements to communications fit.

**Modernisation:** All being modernised under Delex programme 1983-86 with new air radar, GFC, communications and EW equipment. The Bofors rocket launcher to be replaced by Super RBOC and Tacan to be fitted on a pole mast replacing the top section of the lattice mast. Triple Mark 32 torpedo tubes to be fitted. Extension until 1991-94. Cost $22 million per ship.

*Improved Restigouche class ("Gatineau") 10/1985 (Dr. Giorgio Arra)*

| | |
|---|---|
| **ROTHESAY** | F 107 |
| **PLYMOUTH** | F 126 |

**Displacement, tons:** 2 380 standard; 2 800 full load
**Dimensions, feet (metres):** 370 × 41 × 17.3 *(112.8 × 12.5 × 5.3)*
**Aircraft:** 1 Wasp helicopter
**Missiles:** SAM; Seacat (quad launcher)
**Guns:** 2—4.5 in *(115 mm)*/45 (twin Mk 6)
**A/S weapons:** 1—3-barrelled Mk 10 mortar
**Main engines:** 2 double reduction geared turbines; 2 shafts; 30 000 shp
**Boilers:** 2 Babcock & Wilcox
**Speed, knots:** 30
**Oil fuel, tons:** 400
**Complement:** 235 (15 officers and 220 ratings) *(Rothesay)*; 244 (16 officers and 228 ratings) *(Plymouth)*
**Commissioned:** 1960-71

Provided under the 1954-55 programme. Originally basically similar to the 'Whitby' class but with modifications in layout.

**Class:** Remaining ships likely to survive until 1988.

**Modernisation:** The 'Rothesay' class was reconstructed and modernised from 1966-72 during which time they were equipped to operate a Westland Wasp helicopter armed with homing torpedoes. A flight deck and hangar were built on aft, necessitating the removal of one of their anti-submarine mortars. A Seacat replaced the 40 mm gun.

*Rothesay class ("Brighton" now deleted) 4/1977 (C & S Taylor)*

| | |
|---|---|
| SAGUENAY | 206 |
| SKEENA | 207 |
| OTTAWA | 229 |
| MARGAREE | 230 |
| FRASER | 233 |
| ASSINIBOINE | 234 |

**Displacement, tons:** 2 260 standard; 3 051 full load (after conversion)
**Dimensions, feet (metres):** 366 × 42 × 14 (hull) *(111.6 × 12.8 × 4.3)*
**Aircraft:** 1 CHSS-2 Sea King helicopter
**Guns:** 2—3 in *(76 mm)*/50 (twin Mk 33)
**A/S weapons:** 1 Mk 10 Limbo in after well; 2 triple Mk 32 torpedo tubes for Mk 44 or 46 torpedoes
**Main engines:** 2 English Electric geared turbines; 2 shafts; 30 000 shp
**Boilers:** 2 Babcock and Wilcox water tube
**Speed, knots:** 28
**Range, miles:** 4 570 at 12 knots
**Complement:** 213 (16 officers, 197 ratings) (plus air unit of 7 officers and 13 ratings)
**Commissioned:** 1956-57

The first major warships to be designed in Canada—much assistance was received from the Royal Navy (propelling machinery of British design) and the US Navy.
*St. Laurent* declared surplus in 1974 and disposed of in 1979. Sank under tow to breakers' yard.

**Modernisation:** All modernised under Delex programme 1979-82 although no new sensors have been included. Extension until 1987-90.

*St. Laurent class ("Skeena") 4/1985*
*(L & L van Ginderen)*

| | |
|---|---|
| **TROMP** | F 801 |
| **DE RUYTER** | F 806 |

**Displacement, tons:** 3 665 standard; 4 308 full load

**Dimensions, feet (metres):** 454 × 48.6 × 15.1 *(138.4 × 14.8 × 4.6)*

**Aircraft:** 1 Lynx helicopter

**Missiles:** SSM; Harpoon (eight single cells) (16 missiles) SAM; SM-1 (single Mk 13 launcher) (40 missiles) SAM; Sea Sparrow (octuple launcher) (16 missiles)

**Guns:** 2—4.7 in *(120 mm)*/50 (twin Bofors)

**A/S weapons:** 6 (2 triple) Mk 32 ASW torpedo tubes

**Main engines:** 2 Olympus gas turbines; 50 000 hp; 2 Tyne cruising gas turbines; 8 000 hp

**Speed, knots:** 30

**Fuel, tons:** 630

**Range, miles:** 5 000 at 18 knots

**Complement:** 306

**Commissioned:** 1975-76

First design allowance was voted for in 1967 estimates. Ordered (announced on 27 July 1970) for laying down in 1971. Hangar and helicopter landing platform aft. Fitted as flagships.

**Midlife conversions:** Scheduled for 1988-90.

*Tromp class ("Tromp") 8/1981*
*(Wright & Logan)*

| | |
|---|---|
| ISAAC SWEERS | F 814 |
| EVERTSEN | F 815 |

**Displacement, tons:** 2 255 standard; 2 835 full
load
**Dimensions, feet (metres):** 372 × 41 × 13.8
*(113.4 × 12.5 × 4.2)*
**Aircraft:** 1 Lynx helicopter
**Missiles:** SSM; 8 Harpoon SAM; Seacat (2 quad
launchers)
**Gun:** 1—76 mm/62 (single Compact)
**A/S weapons:** 6 (2 triple) Mk 32 torpedo tubes
**Main engines:** 2 double reduction geared
turbines; 2 shafts; 30 000 shp
**Boilers:** 2 Babcock & Wilcox (fully automated)
**Speed, knots:** 28.5
**Range, miles:** 4 500 at 12 knots
**Complement:** 180 (after modernisation)
**Commissioned:** 1967-68

Ordered in 1964. Four to be transferred to
Indonesia between October 1986 and 1988—all
sold to Indonesia 10 February 1986 with an
interest shown in the surviving pair. All to be
refitted and supplied with full spares but no
helicopter.

**Design:** Although in general these ships are
based on the design of the British Improved Type
12 ('Leander' class), there are a number of
modifications to suit the requirements of the
Royal Netherlands Navy. As far as possible
equipment of Netherlands' manufacture was
installed. This resulted in a number of changes in
the ship's superstructure compared with the
British 'Leander' class.

**Modernisation:** These ships underwent mid-life
modernisation at Rykswerf Den Helder in 1979-
83. This included replacement of 4.5 in turret by
76 mm, A/S mortar by torpedo tubes, new
electronics and electrics, updating of Ops. Room
by ADP, improved communications, extensive
automation with reduction in complement,
enlarged hangar for Lynx and improved
habitability.

*Van Speijk class ("Evertsen")*
*9/1985 (W. Sartori)*

| | |
|---|---|
| WIELINGEN | F 910 |
| WESTDIEP | F 911 |
| WANDELAAR | F 912 |
| WESTHINDER | F 913 |

**Displacement, tons:** 1 940 light; 2 430 full load
**Dimensions, feet (metres):** 349 × 40.3 × 18.4 *(106.4 × 12.3 × 5.6)*
**Missiles:** SAM; Sea Sparrow (1—8 cell launcher) SSM; MM 38 Exocet (4 launchers)
**Guns:** 1—3.9 in *(100 mm)*/55 Mod 1968 3; provision for 1 CIWS
**Torpedo launchers:** 2 for L-5 torpedoes
**A/S rocket launchers:** 1—6-barrelled 375 mm Creusot- Loire with Bofors rockets
**Rocket launchers:** 2—Super RBOC dual-purpose Chaff/flare launchers
**Main engines:** CODOG—1 Rolls-Royce Olympus TM3B gas turbine; 28 000 bhp; 2 Cockerill CO-240 V12 2400 diesels; 6 000 bhp. Twin cp propellers
**Speed, knots:** 29 (15 on 1 diesel, 20 on 2 diesels)
**Range, miles:** 4 500 at 18 knots; 6 000 at 15 knots
**Complement:** 160 (15 officers; 145 men)
**Based:** Zeebrugge
**Commissioned:** 1978

This compact, well-armed class of frigate is the first class fully designed by the Belgian Navy and built in Belgian yards. All fitted with hull-mounted sonar and fin stabilisers. Fully air-conditioned.

*Wielingen class ("Weilingen")*
*6/1983 (*L & L van Ginderen*)*

| | |
|---|---|
| AQUILA | F 542 |
| ALBATROS | F 543 |
| ALCIONE | F 544 |
| AIRONE | F 545 |

**Displacement, tons:** 800 standard; 950 full load
**Dimensions, feet (metres):** 250.3 × 31.5 × 9.2
  *(76.3 × 9.6 × 2.8)*
**Guns:** 2—40 mm/70 Bofors
**A/S weapons:** 2 Hedgehogs Mk II; 2 DCTs; 1 DC
  rack; 6 (2 triple) US Mk 32 A/S torpedo tubes
**Main engines:** 2 Fiat diesels; 2 shafts; 5 200 bhp
**Speed, knots:** 19
**Oil fuel, tons:** 100
**Range, miles:** 5 000 at 18 knots
**Complement:** 99
**Commissioned:** 1955-56

Eight ships of this class were built in Italy under
US offshore MDAP orders; three for Italy, four for
Denmark (since deleted) and one for the
Netherlands. *Aquila* was transferred to the Italian
Navy on 18 October 1961 at Den Helder from the
Netherlands Navy.

*Albatros class ("Airone") 6/1980*
*(Achille Rastelli)*

**PIETRO DE CRISTOFARO**

|                        |       |
|------------------------|-------|
|                        | F 540 |
| **UMBERTO GROSSO**     | F 541 |
| **LICIO VISINTINI**    | F 546 |
| **SALVATORE TODARO**   | F 550 |

**Displacement, tons:** 850 standard; 1 020 full load
**Dimensions, feet (metres):** 263.2 × 33.7 × 9 *(80.2 × 10.3 × 2.7)*
**Guns:** 2—3 in *(76 mm)*/62 (single MM 1)
**A/S weapons:** 1 single semi-automatic DC mortar Mk 113; 2 triple US Mk 32 A/S torpedo tubes
**Main engines:** 2 Fiat 3012 RSS diesels; 2 shafts; 8 400 bhp
**Speed, knots:** 23
**Oil fuel, tons:** 95
**Range, miles:** 4 000 at 16 knots
**Complement:** 131 (8 officers, 123 men)
**Commissioned:** 1965-66

The design is an improved version of the 'Albatros' class.

*De Cristofaro* converted for other duties—VDS removed.

*De Cristofaro class ("Pietro de Cristofaro") 1981 (*Commander Aldo Fraccaroli*)*

**HANS BÜRKNER**      A 1449

**Displacement, tons:** 1 000 full load
**Dimensions, feet (metres):** 265.2 × 30.8 × 9.2
*(81 × 9.4 × 2.8)*
**A/S weapons:** 1—4-barrelled DC mortar; 2 DC racks;
2—21 in *(533 mm)* torpedo tubes
**Main engines:** 4 MAN diesels; 2 shafts; 13 600 shp = 19.5 knots
**Complement:** 50
**Commissioned:** 1963

Launched on 16 July 1961. Named after designer of German First World War battleships (1909-18). General purpose utility vessel manned by civilians for trials.

*Hans Bürkner, 6/1983. (*Stefan Terzibaschitsch*)*

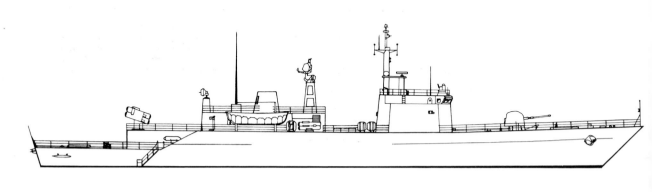

**MINERVA**
**URANIA**
**DANAIDE**
**SFINGE**
**CHIMERA**
**DRIADE**
**FENICE**
**SIBILLA**

**Displacement, tons:** 1 285 full load
**Dimensions, feet (metres):** 284.4 × 33.8 × 18 *(87 × 10.3 × 5.5)*
**Missiles:** SAM; 1 Albatros system (8 cell)
**Gun:** 1—3 in *(76 mm)*/62 OTO Melara Super Rapido
**A/S weapons:** 6 ILAS 3 A/S torpedo tubes (2 triple)
**Main engines:** 2 GMT 230.20 DVM diesels; 2 shafts; 11 600 hp = 25 knots
**Range, miles:** 3 500 at 18 knots
**Complement:** 121 (9 officers, 112 ratings)
**Commissioned:** First due 1986

First four ordered from CNR (Riva Trigoso/Muggiano) in November 1982. Designed as inexpensive ships with a number of peacetime roles—EEZ patrol, fishery protection, COs training and the like. Building time to be 28 months.

*'Minerva' class (*Lt Cdr Erminio Bagnasco*)*

| | |
|---|---|
| **SLEIPNER** | F 310 |
| **AEGER** | F 311 |

**Displacement, tons:** 600 standard; 780 full load
**Dimensions, feet (metres):** 227.5 × 27.2 × 9
  *(69.4 × 8.3 × 2.7)*
**Guns:** 1—3 in *(76 mm)* (US Mk 34 mount);
  1—40 mm
**A/S weapons:** Terne ASW system; (2 triple) Mk
  32 torpedo tubes
**Mines:** Laying capability
**Main engines:** 4 Maybach (MTU) diesels; 2
  shafts; 8 800 bhp = over 20 knots
**Complement:** 63
**Commissioned:** 1965-67

Under the five-year programme only two instead
of the originally planned five corvettes were built.

**Modernisation:** Similar changes planned to
those under 'Oslo Class'.

*Sleipner class ("Aeger") 8/1981*
*(Michael D. J. Lennon)*

| | |
|---|---|
| **THETIS** | P 6052 |
| **HERMES** | P 6053 |
| **NAJADE** | P 6054 |
| **TRITON** | P 6055 |
| **THESEUS** | P 6056 |

**Displacement, tons:** 732 full load
**Dimensions, feet (metres):** 229.7 × 27 × 14 *(70 × 8.5 × 4.2)*
**Guns:** 2—Breda 40 mm/L70 (twin mounting)
**A/S weapons:** Bofors 375 mm 4-barrelled DC mortar; DC rails
**Torpedo tubes:** 4—21 in *(533 mm)*
**Main engines:** 2 MAN diesels; 2 shafts; 6 800 bhp = 19.5 knots
**Complement:** 64 (4 officers and 60 men)
**Commissioned:** 1961-63

*Thetis class ("Thetis") 8/1982 (*L & L van Ginderen*)*

**FEARLESS**  L 10
**INTREPID**  L 11

**Displacement, tons:** 11 060 standard; 12 120 full load; 16 950 dock flooded

**Dimensions, feet (metres):** 500 wl; 520 oa × 80 × 20.5 (keel) *(152.4; 158.5 × 24.4 × 6.2)*

**Draught, flooded:** 32 *(9.8)* aft; 23 *(7)* fwd

**Landing craft:** 4 LCUs in dock; 4 LCVP at davits

**Vehicles:** Specimen load: 15 tanks, seven 3 ton and 20 quarter-ton trucks

**Aircraft:** Flight deck facilities for 5 Wessex helicopters

**Missiles:** SAM; Seacat (4 quad launchers) *(Fearless)*; 2 launchers *(Intrepid)*

**Guns:** 2—40 mm/70 Bofors; in addition 2—30 mm and 2—20 mm BMARC in *Intrepid*

**Main engines:** 2 EE turbines; 2 shafts; 22 000 shp

**Boilers:** 2 Babcock & Wilcox

**Speed, knots:** 21

**Range, miles:** 5 000 at 20 knots

**Complement:** 550 (50 officers, 500 ratings or marines)

**Commissioned:** 1965-67

Landing craft are floated through the open stern by flooding compartments of the ship and lowering her in the water. The helicopter platform is also the deckhead of the dock.

In 1981 their impending deletion was announced—*Intrepid* in 1982 and *Fearless* in 1984. In February 1982 it was reported that they were to be reprieved.

In January 1984 *Intrepid* began a refit at Devonport until June 1985. *Fearless* to reserve mid 1985.

*"Fearless"*

| | |
|---|---|
| **IWO JIMA** | LPH 2 |
| **OKINAWA** | LPH 3 |
| **GUADALCANAL** | LPH 7 |
| **GUAM** | LPH 9 |
| **TRIPOLI** | LPH 10 |
| **NEW ORLEANS** | LPH 11 |
| **INCHON** | LPH 12 |

**Displacement, tons:** 11 000 (2, 3 and 7), 11 755 (9), 11 877 (10), 11 432 (11), 10 722 (12) light; 18 042 (2), 18 154 (3), 18 000 (7), 18 300 (9), 18 515 (10), 18 241 (11), 18 825 (12) full load

**Dimensions, feet (metres):** 602.3 × 84 × 26 *(183.7 × 25.6 × 7.9)*

**Flight deck width, feet (metres):** 104 *(31.7)*

**Aircraft:** For helicopters see *Aircraft* note 4 AV-8A Harriers in place of some troop helicopters

**Missiles:** SAM; 2 Sea Sparrow launchers (Mk 25) (BPDMS) (except LPH 2, 3, 7 and 9)

**Guns:** 4—3 in *(76 mm)*/50 (twin Mk 33); 2—20 mm Mk 16 CIWS (to be fitted—already in LPH 2, 3, 7 and 9)

**Main engines:** 1 geared turbine (De Laval in *Tripoli,* GE in *Inchon,* Westinghouse in others); 1 shaft; 22 000 shp

**Boilers:** 2 Babcock & Wilcox in *Guam;* Combustion Engineering in remainder

**Speed, knots:** 23

**Complement:** 754 (55 officers, 699 enlisted men)

**Troops:** 1 746 (144 officers, 1 602 enlisted men)

**Commissined:** 1961-70

*Iwo Jima* was the world's first ship designed specifically to operate helicopters. Each LPH can carry a Marine battalion landing team, its guns, vehicles, and equipment, plus a reinforced squadron of transport helicopters and various support personnel.

*Guam* was modified late in 1971 and began operations in January 1972 as an interim sea control ship. She operated Harrier AV-8A V/STOL aircraft and SH-3 Sea King A/S helicopters in convoy escort exercises; she reverted to the amphibious role in 1974 but kept 12 AV-8As on board.

Scheduled to be replaced by 'Wasp' class LHDs starting in the 1990s. To receive limited SLEP.

**Aircraft:** The flight decks provide for simultaneous take off or landing of seven CH-46 Sea Knight or four CH-53 Sea Stallion helicopters during normal operations. The hangar decks can accommodate 20 CH-46 Sea Knight or 11 CH-53 Sea Stallion helicopters, or various combinations of helicopters.

*Iwo Jima class ("Okinawa") 6/1985 (Dr. Giorgio Arra)*

| | |
|---|---|
| **TARAWA** | LHA 1 |
| **SAIPAN** | LHA 2 |
| **BELLEAU WOOD** | LHA 3 |
| **NASSAU** | LHA 4 |
| **PELILEU** (ex-*Da Nang*) | LHA 5 |

**Displacement, tons:** 39 300 full load
**Dimensions, feet (metres):** 820 × 106 × 26 *(250 × 32.3 × 7.9)*
**Flight deck, feet (metres):** 118.1 *(36)*
**Aircraft:** (See *Aircraft* note for helicopters). Harrier AV-8A V/STOL aircraft in place of some helicopters as required
**Missiles:** SAM—2 Sea Sparrow launchers (Mk 25) (BPDMS)
**Guns:** 3—5 in *(127 mm)*/54 (single Mk 45); 2—20 mm Mk 16 Phalanx CIWS (already in *Saipan*); 6—20 mm (Mk 67) (single); 2—40 mm saluting
**Main engines:** 2 geared turbines (Westinghouse); 2 shafts; 70 000 shp
**Boilers:** 2 Combustion Engineering
**Speed, knots:** 24
**Range, miles:** 10 000 at 20 knots
**Complement:** 935 (56 officers, 879 enlisted men)
**Troops:** 1 703
**Commissioned:** 1976-80

Originally intended to be a class of nine ships. LHA 1 was authorised in the FY 1969 new construction programme, the LHA 2 and LHA 3 in FY 1970 and LHA 4 and LHA 5 in FY 1971. All ships of this class were built at a new ship production facility known as 'Ingalls West'. The new yard was developed specifically for multi-ship construction of the same design. LHA 5 renamed 15 February 1978.

**Aircraft:** The flight deck can operate a maximum of 9 CH-53 Sea Stallion or 12 CH-46 Sea Knight helicopters; the hangar deck can accommodate 19 CH-53 Sea Stallion or 26 CH-46 Sea Knight helicopters. A mix of these and other helicopters and at times AV-8A Harriers could be embarked except in LHA 1.

*Tarawa class ("Tarawa") 1/1985*
*(L & L van Ginderen)*

| BARCELÓ | PC 11 |
|---|---|
| LAYA | PC 12 |
| JAVIER QUIROGA | PC 13 |
| ORDÓÑEZ | PC 14 |
| ACEVEDO | PC 15 |
| CÁNDIDO PÉREZ | PC 16 |

**Displacement, tons:** 134 full load
**Dimensions, feet (metres):** 118.7 ×19 ×6.2 *(36.2 × 5.8 × 1.9)*
**Guns:** 1—40 mm Breda Bofors 350; 1—20 mm Oerlikon GAM 204; 2—12.7 mm
**Torpedo tubes:** Provision for 2—21 in *(533 mm)*
**Main engines:** 2 MTU-Bazán MD-16V TB 90 diesels; 2 shafts; 5 760 bhp
**Speed, knots:** 36; 20 cruising
**Range, miles:** 1 200 at 17 knots
**Complement:** 19
**Commissioned:** 1976-77

Ordered 5 December 1973, the prototype, *Barceló*, being built by Lürssen, Vegesack with MTU engines. All manned by the Navy although the cost is being borne by the Ministry of Commerce. Of Lürssen TNC 36 design.

**Missiles:** Reported as able to take two or four surface- to-surface missiles instead of 20 mm gun and torpedo tubes.

**Pennant numbers:** Some carry PC, some P on the bow.

*Barcelo class ("Javier Quiroga")*
*8/1981 (*Dr. Giorgio Arra*)*

**GIRNE**                       P 140

**Displacement, tons:** 341 standard; 399 full load
**Dimensions, feet (metres):** 190.6 × 24.9 × 9.2
 *(58.1 × 7.6 × 2.8)*
**Guns:** 2—40 mm (single); 2—20 mm
**A/S weapons:** 2 Mousetraps Mk 20; 2 DCTs; 2
 DC racks
**Main engines:** 2 MTU diesels; 2 shafts; 9 000 hp
 = 36 knots
**Range, miles:** 4 200 at 16 knots
**Complement:** 30 (3 officers, 27 ratings)
**Commissioned:** 1976

Originally first of a series. Project now cancelled.
Has US Mk 51 optical director.

*Girne class ("Girne") 3/1983*
*(Hartmut Ehlers)*

| | |
|---|---|
| HAUK | P 986 |
| ØRN | P 987 |
| TERNE | P 988 |
| TJELD | P 989 |
| SKARV | P 990 |
| TEIST | P 991 |
| JO | P 992 |
| LOM | P 993 |
| STEGG | P 994 |
| FALK | P 995 |
| RAVN | P 996 |
| GRIBB | P 997 |
| GEIR | P 998 |
| ERLE | P 999 |

**Displacement, tons:** 120 standard; 148 full load
**Dimensions, feet (metres):** 120 × 20 × 5 *(36.5 × 6.1 × 1.5)*
**Missiles:** SSM; 6 Penguin Mk 2 (single launchers)
**Guns:** 1—40 mm; 1—20 mm
**Torpedo tubes:** 2—21 in *(533 mm)*
**Main engines:** 2 MTU diesels; 7 200 hp = 32 knots
**Range, miles:** 440 at 34 knots
**Complement:** 20
**Commissioned:** 1977-80

Ordered 12 June 1975—ten from Bergens Mek. Verksteder (Laksevag) (also building Swedish 'Hugin' class) and four from Westamarin. Very similar to 'Snögg' class with improved fire control.

*Hauk class ("Stegg") (Royal Norwegian Navy)*

## GREECE

| | |
|---|---|
| **HESPEROS** (ex-*Seeadler*) | P 50 |
| **KENTAUROS** (ex-*Habicht*) | P 52 |
| **KYKLON** (ex-*Greif*) | P 53 |
| **LELAPS** (ex-*Kondor*) | P 54 |
| **SKORPIOS** (ex-*Kormoran*) | P 55 |
| **TYFON** (ex-*Geier*) | P 56 |

## TURKEY

| | |
|---|---|
| **FIRTINA** (ex-*Pelikan*) | P 330 |
| **TUFAN** (ex-*Storch*) | P 331 |
| **MIZRAK** (ex-*Hähner*) | P 333 |
| **KALKAN** (ex-*Wolf*) | P 335 |
| **KARAYEL** (ex-*Pinguin*) | P 336 |

## TURKEY
## LARGE PATROL CRAFT
## Ex-GFR 'ZOBEL' CLASS

**Number in class:** 6

(ex-*Gepard*)
(ex-*Frettchen*)
(ex-*Dachs*)
(ex-*Weisel*)
(ex-*Ozelot*)
(ex-*Huäne*)

*Jaguar class ("Firtina") (*Reiner
Nerlich*)*

**Displacement, tons:** 160 standard; 190 full load
**Dimensions, feet (metres):** 139.4 × 23.6 × 7.9
  *(42.5 × 7.2 × 2.4)*
**Guns:** 2—40 mm Bofors/L70 (single)
**Torpedo tubes:** 4—21 in *(533 mm)*
**Main engines:** 4 diesels; 4 shafts; 12 000 bhp =
  42 knots
**Complement:** 39
**Commissioned:** 1958

## GREECE

Transferred 1976-77. *Kyklon, Tyfon*
commissioned in Hellenic Navy 12 December
1976.

## TURKEY

In late 1975-early 1976 seven 'Jaguar' class
were transferred by Federal Germany to Turkey.
In addition three more were transferred for spare
parts.
   The ex-'Zobel' class large patrol craft are
conversions of the 'Jaguar' class transferred in
1984, last three on 8 October 1984.
   Carry only two torpedo tubes.

**DENIZKUSU** (ex-*P 336*)          P 321
**ATMACA** (ex-*P 335*)            P 322
**SAHIN** (ex-*P 334*)             P 323
**KARTAL** (ex-*P 333*)            P 324
**PELIKAN**                        P 326
**ALBATROS** (ex-*P 325*)          P 327
**ŞIMŞEK** (ex-*P 332*)            P 328
**KASIRGA** (ex-*P 338*)           P 329

**Displacement, tons:** 160 standard; 180 full load
**Dimensions, feet (metres):** 140.5 × 23.5 × 7.2
   *(42.8 × 7.1 × 2.2)*
**Missiles:** SSM; 4—Penguin 2
**Guns:** 2—40 mm/70 (single)
**Torpedo tubes:** 2—21 in *(533 mm)*
**Main engines:** 4 MTU 16V 538 (Maybach)
   diesels; 4 shafts; 12 000 bhp = 42 knots
**Complement:** 39
**Commissioned:** 1967-68

Of the Federal German Jaguar type, built in
Germany, *Meltem* sunk in collision with Soviet
freighter in Bosphorus in October 1985.
Subsequently salvaged but probably beyond
repair.

*Kartal class ("Meltem") 1978 (*Selçuk
Emre*)*

**ANTHIPOPLOIARHOS ANNINOS**
(ex-*Navsithoi*)                                   P 14
**IPOPLOIARHOS ARLIOTIS**
(ex-*Evniki*)                                       P 15
**IPOPLOIARHOS KONIDIS**
(ex-*Kymothoi*)                                   P 16
**IPOPLOIARHOS BATSIS** (ex-*Calypso*) P 17

**Displacement, tons:** 234 standard; 255 full load
**Dimensions, feet (metres):** 154.2 × 23.3 × 8.2
    *(47 × 7.1 × 2.5)*
**Missiles:** SSM; 4 Exocet MM38 (single cells)
**Guns:** 4—35 mm/90 (twin Oerlikon)
**Torpedo tubes:** 2 aft for 21 in *(533 mm)* FDR
    wire-guided torpedoes
**Main engines:** 4 MTU diesels; 4 shafts; 12 000
    bhp = 36.5 knots
**Oil fuel, tons:** 39
**Range, miles:** 850 at 25 knots
**Complement:** 40 (4 officers, and 36 men)
**Commissioned:** 1971-72

Ordered in 1969. Fitted with Thomson-CSF Triton
radar and Plessey IFF Mk 10. *I. Arliotis* launched
8 September 1971. *A. Anninos* launched 20
December 1971. *I. Batsis* launched 27 April
1971. *I. Konidis* launched 26 January 1972.
All built in France.

*La Combattante II class*
*(''Anthipoploiarhos Anninos'') 1980*
*(D. Dervissis)*

| | |
|---|---|
| **ANTIPLOIARHOS LASKOS** | P 20 |
| **PLOTARHIS BLESSAS** | P 21 |
| **IPOPLOIARHOS MIKONIOS** | P 22 |
| **IPOPLOIARHOS TROUPAKIS** | P 23 |
| **SIMEOFOROS KAVALOUDIS** | P 24 |
| **ANTHIPOPLOIARHOS KOSTAKOS** | P 25 |
| **IPOPLOIARHOS DEYIANNIS** | P 26 |
| **SIMEOFOROS XENOS** | P 27 |
| **SIMEOFOROS SIMITZOPOULOS** | P 28 |
| **SIMEOFOROS STARAKIS** | P 29 |

**Displacement, tons:** 359 standard; 425 full load (first four); 329 standard; 429 full load (second group)

**Dimensions, feet (metres):** 184 × 26.2 × 7 *(56.2 × 8 × 2.1)*

**Missiles:** SSM; 4 Exocet MM 38 (single cells) (first four); SSM; 6 Penguin II (second group)

**Guns:** 2—76 mm/62 (single Compact); 4— 30 mm Emerlec (twin)

**Torpedo tubes:** 2—21 in *(533 mm)* (aft) for wire-guided torpedoes

**Main engines:** 4 MTU MD20V 538 TB 91 diesels; 4 shafts; 18 000 bhp = 35.7 knots

**Range, miles:** 700 at 32.6 knots; 2 000 at 15 knots

**Complement:** 42 (5 officers, 37 ratings)

**Commissioned:** 1977-81

First four ordered in September 1974 and built in France. *A. Laskos* laid down 28 June 1975, launched 6 July 1976; *P. Blessas* laid down 28 October 1975, launched 10 November 1976; *I. Troupakis* laid down 27 January 1976, launched 25 January 1977, *I. Mikonios* laid down 7 April 1976, launched 5 May 1977. Second group of six ordered 1978, first pair laid down mid-1978. *S. Kavaloudis* launched 10 November 1979, *A. Kostakos* 1 March 1980, *I. Deyiannis* 14 July 1980 and *S. Xenos* 8 September 1980, last pair in 1981. All six built in Greece.

*La Combattante III class (*"Plotarhis Blessas"*)*

| | |
|---|---|
| **LAZAGA** | PC 01 |
| **ALSEDO** | PC 02 |
| **CADARSO** | PC 03 |
| **VILLAMIL** | PC 04 |
| **BONIFAZ** | PC 05 |
| **RECALDE** | PC 06 |

**Displacement, tons:** 275 standard; 399 full load
**Dimensions, feet (metres):** 190.6 × 24.9 × 8.5
*(58.1 × 7.6 × 2.6)*
**Missiles:** See note
**Guns:** 1—3 in *(76 mm)*/L62 (Compact); 1—
40 mm/L70 Breda Bofors 350P; 2—20 mm
Oerlikon GK 204
**A/S weapons:** Provision for 2 triple Mk 32
torpedo tube mountings and DC racks
**Main engines:** 2 MTU-Bazán MA15 TB91
diesels; 8 000 bhp
**Speed, knots:** 30
**Range, miles:** 6 100 at 17 knots
**Complement:** 34 (4 officers, 30 ratings)
**Commissioned:** 1975-77

Ordered in 1972, primarily for Fishery Protection
duties. Although all are operated by the Navy half
the cost is being borne by the Ministry of
Commerce. Of similar hull form to Israeli 'Reshef'
class and to 'S-143' class of Federal Germany
and of basic Lürssen Type 57 design but with only
two engines.
   *Lazaga* was steamed to Spain in April 1975 for
equipping and arming.

**Appearance:** A mast which is abaft and higher
than the radome has been fitted, probably for
ESM.

**Missiles:** To receive twin or quad Harpoon in
1985, without change of gun armament.

**Pennant numbers:** Some carry PC, some P on the
bow.

*Lazaga class ("Villamil") 1/1985*
*(L & L van Ginderen)*

| | |
|---|---|
| **DOĞAN** | P 340 |
| **MARTI** | P 341 |
| **TAYFUN** | P 342 |
| **VOLKAN** | P 343 |
| **RÜZGAR** | P 344 |
| **POYRAZ** | P 345 |

**Displacement, tons:** 436 full load
**Dimensions, feet (metres):** 190.6 × 25 × 8.8
  *(58.1 × 7.6 × 2.7)*
**Missiles:** SSM; 8 Harpoon (2 quad launchers)
**Guns:** 1—76 mm; 2—35 mm/90 Oerlikon (twin
  aft)
**Main engines:** 4—16-cyl MTU diesels; 18 000 hp
  = 38 knots
**Range, miles:** 700 at 35 knots
**Complement:** 38
**Commissioned:** 1977-85

First four ordered 3 August 1973.

*Lürssen FPB 57 type ("Volkan")*
*11/1983 (*L & L Ginderen*)*

| | |
|---|---|
| **L'AUDACIEUSE** | P 682 |
| **LA BOUDEUSE** | P 683 |
| **LA CAPRICIEUSE** | P 684 |
| **LA FOUGEUSE** | P 685 |
| **LA GLORIEUSE** | P 686 |
| **LA GRACIEUSE** | P 687 |
| **LA MOQUEUSE** | P 688 |
| **LA RAILLEUSE** | P 689 |
| **LA RIEUSE** | P 690 |
| **LA TAPAGEUSE** | P 691 |

**Displacement, tons:** 423 full load
**Dimensions, feet (metres):** 177.2 × 26.2 × 8.5
 *(54 × 8 × 2.5)*
**Missiles:** (see notes)
**Guns:** 1—40 mm; 1—20 mm
**Main engines:** 2—16-cyl SEMT-Pielstick 16PA4
 V200 VGDS diesels; 2 shafts (cp propellers);
 8 000 hp
**Speed, knots:** 24
**Range, miles:** 4 000 at 15 knots
**Complement:** 25 + 20 passengers
**Commissioned:** 1985-

First four ordered in May 1982, two more in 1983 with further four in January 1984. 682-689 will operate abroad.

**Commissioning:** The original engines of this class have been unsatisfactory. Replacements have been ordered and construction has been slowed. Those completed have been laid up at Lorient until new engines are available.

**Design:** Steel hull and superstructure protected by an upper deck bulwark. Design modified from original missile craft configuration. Now capable of transporting personnel with appropriate store-rooms. Of more robust construction than previously planned—to be used as overseas transports. Can be converted for missile armament (MM 38) with dockyard assistance.

**Missiles:** In later ships Sadral SAM will replace 20 mm gun. To be retro-fitted in earlier ships.

*P 400 class ("l'Audacieuse")*
*8/1985 (Jean Robert)*

| | |
|---|---|
| **TRIDENT** | P 670 |
| **GLAIVE** | P 671 |
| **PERTUISANE** | P 673 |

**Displacement, tons:** 115 standard; 130 full load
**Dimensions, feet (metres):** 121.4 × 18 × 5.2 *(37 × 5.5 × 1.6)*
**Missiles:** 6—SS 12
**Guns:** 1—40 mm; 1—12.7 mm
**Main engines:** 2 AGO diesels; 2 shafts (cp propellers); 4 000 hp = 26 knots
**Range, miles:** 1 750 at 10 knots; 750 at 20 knots
**Complement:** 18 (1 officer and 17 men)
**Commissioned:** 1976-77

These were intended as lead boats for a class of 30 in 'Plan Bleu' of which 16 were to be adapted for overseas service. Like other craft of similar size they have proved too small for their intended role. All to join Gendarmerie after relief by P 400s.
**Deployment:** Atlantic, *Glaive, Pertuisane.* West Indies, *Trident.*

**Note:** All of this class to be transferred, possibly in 1986-87 when relieved by 'P 400' class (q.v.).

*Patra class ("Pertuisane") 4/1983*
*(W. Sartori)*

| | |
|---|---|
| **SNÖGG** (ex-*Lyr*) | P 980 |
| **RAPP** | P 981 |
| **SNAR** | P 982 |
| **RASK** | P 983 |
| **KVIKK** | P 984 |
| **KJAPP** | P 985 |

**Displacement, tons:** 100 standard; 135 full load
**Dimensions, feet (metres):** 120 × 20 × 5 *(36.5 × 6.1 × 1.3)*
**Missiles:** SSM; 4 Penguin (single launchers)
**Gun:** 1—40 mm
**Torpedo tubes:** 4—21 in *(533 mm)*
**Main engines:** 2 Maybach (MTU) diesels; 2 shafts; 7 200 bhp = 32 knots
**Complement:** 19
**Commissioned:** 1970-71

Steel hulled fast attack craft, started coming into service in 1970. Hulls are similar to those of the 'Storm' class gunboats. Modernisation of fire control and electronics due in about 1990.

*Snögg class, 1985 (*Royal Norwegian Navy*)*

| | |
|---|---|
| SØLØVEN | P 510 |
| SØRIDDEREN | P 511 |
| SØBJØRNEN | P 512 |
| SØHESTEN | P 513 |
| SØHUNDEN | P 514 |
| SØULVEN | P 515 |

**Displacement, tons:** 95 standard; 120 full load
**Dimensions, feet (metres):** 99 × 26.2 × 8.2 *(30.3 × 8 × 2.5)*
**Gun:** 1—40 mm Bofors
**Torpedo tubes:** 2 or 4—21 in *(533 mm)*
**Main engines:** 3 Bristol Siddeley Proteus gas turbines; 3 shafts; 12 750 bhp = 54 knots
2 General Motors diesels on wing shafts for cruising; 300 bhp = 10 knots
**Range, miles:** 400 at 46 knots
**Complement:** 25
**Commissioned:** 1965-67

*Soloven class ("Soloven") 6/1985*
*(L & L van Ginderen)*

| | |
|---|---|
| **STORM** | P 960 |
| **BLINK** | P 961 |
| **GLIMT** | P 962 |
| **SKJOLD** | P 963 |
| **TRYGG** | P 964 |
| **KJEKK** | P 965 |
| **DJERV** | P 966 |
| **SKUDD** | P 967 |
| **ARG** | P 968 |
| **STEIL** | P 969 |
| **BRANN** | P 970 |
| **TROSS** | P 971 |
| **HVASS** | P 972 |
| **TRAUST** | P 973 |
| **BROTT** | P 974 |
| **ODD** | P 975 |
| **BRASK** | P 977 |
| **ROKK** | P 978 |
| **GNIST** | P 979 |

**Displacement, tons:** 100 standard; 135 full load
**Dimensions, feet (metres):** 120 × 20 × 5 *(36.5 × 6.1 × 1.5)*
**Missiles:** SSM; 6 Penguin (single launchers)
**Guns:** 1—3 in *(76 mm)*; 1—40 mm
**Main engines:** 2 Maybach (MTU) diesels; 2 shafts; 7 200 bhp = 32 knots
**Complement:** 19
**Commissioned:** 1965-68

The first of 20 (instead of the 23 originally planned) gunboats of a new design built under the five-year programme was *Storm,* launched on 8 February 1963, and completed on 31 May 1963, but this prototype was eventually scrapped and replaced by a new series construction boat as the last of the class.

*Storm class ("Djerv") (*Royal Norwegian Navy*)*

| | |
|---|---|
| SEL | P 343 |
| HVAL | P 348 |
| LAKS | P 349 |
| KNURR | P 357 |
| SKREI | P 380 |
| HAI | P 381 |
| LYR | P 387 |
| DELFIN | P 388 |

**Displacement, tons:** 70 standard; 82 full load
**Dimensions, feet (metres):** 80.3 × 24.5 × 6.8 *(24.5 × 7.5 × 2.1)*
**Guns:** 1—40 mm; 1—20 mm
**Torpedo tubes:** 4—21 in *(533 mm)*
**Main engines:** 2 Napier Deltic Turboblown diesels; 2 shafts; 6 200 bhp = 45 knots
**Range, miles:** 450 at 40 knots; 600 at 25 knots
**Complement:** 18
**Commissioned:** 1960-66

Built of mahogany to Båtservice design, known generally as 'Nasty' class. Some used by Naval Home Guard. Remainder in reserve.

*Hval* ('Tjeld' class) *(Royal Norwegian Navy 1979)*

| | |
|---|---|
| BILLE | P 540 |
| BREDAL | P 541 |
| HAMMER | P 542 |
| HUITFELD | P 543 |
| KRIEGER | P 544 |
| NORBY | P 545 |
| RODSTEEN | P 546 |
| SEHESTED | P 547 |
| SUENSON | P 548 |
| WILLEMOES | P 549 |

**Displacement, tons:** 260 full load
**Dimensions, feet (metres):** 151 × 24 × 8.2 *(46 × 7.4 × 2.5)*
**Missiles:** SSM; 8 Harpoon
**Gun:** 1—76 mm/62 (Compact)
**Torpedo tubes:** 2 or 4—21 in *(533 mm)*
**Main engines:** CODOG; 3 Rolls-Royce Proteus gas turbines; 12 750 bhp; 2 General Motors V 71 diesels for cruising on wing shafts; 1 600 bhp; cp propellers
**Speed, knots:** 38 (12 on diesels)
**Complement:** 25
**Commissioned:** 1976-78

Designed by Lürssen to Danish order. Very similar to Swedish 'Spica II' class (also Lürssen). Original order to Frederikshavn for four boats, increased to eight and finally ten.

*Willemoes* (prototype) laid down in July 1974. Series production began with *Bille* in October 1974.

*Willemoes class ("Hammer")*
*8/1984 (*Ralf Bendfeldt*)*

| | |
|---|---|
| **ALBATROS** | P 6111 |
| **FALKE** | P 6112 |
| **GEIER** | P 6113 |
| **BUSSARD** | P 6114 |
| **SPERBER** | P 6115 |
| **GREIF** | P 6116 |
| **KONDOR** | P 6117 |
| **SEEADLER** | P 6118 |
| **HABICHT** | P 6119 |
| **KORMORAN** | P 6120 |

**Displacement, tons:** 391 full load
**Dimensions, feet (metres):** 189.3 × 24.9 × 8.2 *(57.7 × 7.6 × 2.5)*
**Missiles:** SSM; 4 MM 38 Exocet; SAM (see *Modifications* note)
**Guns:** 2—76 mm OTO Melara (see *Modifications* note)
**Torpedoes:** 2—21 in *(533 mm)* wire guided aft
**Main engines:** 4 MTU diesels; 4 shafts; 18 000 hp = 40 knots (at 23 600 hp) (36 knots continuous)
**Range, miles:** 1 300 at 30 knots
**Complement:** 40
**Commissioned:** 1976-77

AEG-Telefunken main contractor with construction by sub-contractors.

Ordered in 1972 as replacements for last ten boats of the 'Jaguar' class from 1976 onwards. Final funds allocated 13 July 1972. First laid down late 1972. The first boat, *Albatros*, started trials in Dec 1974. Wooden hulled craft.

Names assigned October to December 1981.

**Modifications:** The after 76 mm is being replaced by GD RAM-ASDM SAM system in 1989-90, the guns having been transferred to Type 143A boats. Torpedo tubes are to be removed and a new EW system AEG-Telefunken FL 1800S is to be fitted.

*Habicht* started trials with RAM-ASDM in 1983.

In late 1980s class to have mid-life modernisation to same standard as Type 143A, then to be classified Type 143B.

*Type 143 ("Falke") 5/1983 (L & L van Ginderen)*

| | |
|---|---|
| **TIGER** | P 6141 |
| **ILTIS** | P 6142 |
| **LUCHS** | P 6143 |
| **MARDER** | P 6144 |
| **LEOPARD** | P 6145 |
| **FUCHS** | P 6146 |
| **JAGUAR** | P 6147 |
| **LÖWE** | P 6148 |
| **WOLF** | P 6149 |
| **PANTHER** | P 6150 |
| **HÄHNER** | P 6151 |
| **STORCH** | P 6152 |
| **PELIKAN** | P 6153 |
| **ELSTER** | P 6154 |
| **ALK** | P 6155 |
| **DOMMEL** | P 6156 |
| **WEIHE** | P 6157 |
| **PINGUIN** | P 6158 |
| **REIHER** | P 6159 |
| **KRANICH** | P 6160 |

**Displacement, tons:** 234 standard; 265 full load
**Dimensions, feet (metres):** 154.2 × 23 × 8.9 *(47 × 7 × 2.7)*
**Missiles:** SSM; 4 MM 38 Exocet
**Guns:** 1—76 mm OTO Melara; 1—40 mm Bofors
**Mines:** Laying capability
**Main engines:** 4 MTU diesels; 4 shafts; 12 000 bhp = 36 knots
**Oil fuel, tons:** 38
**Range, miles:** 570 at 30 knots; 1 600 at 15 knots
**Complement:** 30 (4 officers, 26 men)
**Commissioned:** 1972-75

Ordered in December 1970 from DTCN as main contractors. Eight hulls contracted to Lürssen (P 6146, 6148, 6150, 6152, 6154, 6156, 6158, 6160) but all fitted out in France. Steel-hulled craft. Names assigned October to December 1981.

*Type 148 ("Wolf") (Die Bildstelle der Marin)*

# HYDROFOIL 'PEGASUS' TYPE USA

| | |
|---|---|
| PEGASUS | PHM 1 |
| HERCULES | PHM 2 |
| TAURUS | PHM 3 |
| AQUILA | PHM 4 |
| ARIES | PHM 5 |
| GEMINI | PHM 6 |

**Displacement, tons:** 239.6 full load
**Dimensions, feet (metres):**
  foils extended: 132.9 *(40.5)* oa × 28.2 *(8.6)* hull;
  47.5 *(14.5)* over foils × 23.2 *(7.1)* foils retracted:
  145.3 *(44.3)* oa × 28.2 *(8.6)* hull × 7.5 *(2.3)*
**Missiles:** SSM; 8 Harpoon (quad canisters)
**Gun:** 1—76 mm/62 (Mk 75)
**Main engines:** Foilborne; 1 gas turbine (General
  Electric LM 2500); 18 000 shp; Aerojet
  waterjet propulsion units = 48 knots Hullborne;
  2 MTU 8V 331 TC81 diesels; 1 600 bhp; 2
  waterjet propulsion units = 12 knots
**Range, miles:** 1 700 at 9 knots; 700 at 40 knots
**Complement:** 24 (4 officers, 20 enlisted men)
**Commissioned:** 1977-82

The PHM design was developed in conjunction with the Italian and West German navies in an effort to produce a small combatant that would be universally acceptable to NATO navies with minor modifications.

**Classification:** The designation PHM originally was for Patrol Hydrofoil-Missile; reclassified Patrol Combatant Missile (Hydrofoil) on 30 June 1975.

*Pegasus class ("Taurus")*

| | |
|---|---|
| **SPARVIERO** | P 420 |
| **NIBBIO** | P 421 |
| **FALCONE** | P 422 |
| **ASTORE** | P 423 |
| **GRIFONE** | P 424 |
| **GHEPPIO** | P 425 |
| **CONDOR** | P 426 |

**Displacement, tons:** 62.5
**Dimensions, feet (metres):** 80.7 × 39.7 × 14.4
*(24.6 × 12.1 × 4.4)* (length and beam foils
extended, draught hullborne); 75.4 × 22.9 × 5.2
*(23 × 7 × 1.6)* (hull size)
**Missiles:** SSM; 2 Teseo launchers
**Gun:** 1—3 in (76 mm)/62 (Compact)
**Main engines:** Proteus gas turbine driving
waterjet pump; 4 500 bhp; 160 bhp diesel and
retractable propeller unit for hullborne
propulsion
**Speed, knots:** 50 max, 42 cruising (sea state 4);
8 hullborne on diesels
**Range, miles:** 400 at 45 knots; 1 200 at 8 knots
**Complement:** 10 (2 officers, 8 men)
**Commissioned:** 1974-84

*Sparviero* completed for trials 9 May 1973, *Nibbio*
April 1980. *Falcone* laid down May 1977,
launched on 27 October 1980. *Sparviero*
delivered to the Navy as class prototype on 15
July 1974.

*Sparviero class ("Nibbio") 6/1981*
*(Dr. Giorgio Arra)*

| DAPHNE | P 530 |
|--------|-------|
| DRYADEN | P 531 |
| HAVFRUEN | P 533 |
| NAJADEN | P 534 |
| NYMFEN | P 535 |
| NEPTUN | P 536 |
| RAN | P 537 |
| ROTA | P 538 |

**Displacement, tons:** 170
**Dimensions, feet (metres):** 121.3 × 20 × 6.6 *(37 × 6.8 × 2)* (P 530-533)
**Gun:** 1—40 mm plus 2—51 mm flare launchers
**A/S weapons:** DCs
**Main engines:** Two 12-cyl Maybach diesels; 2 shafts; 2 600 bhp = 20 knots (plus 1 cruising 6-cyl Foden diesel; 100 bhp)
**Complement:** 23
**Commissioned:** 1960-65

Four were built under US offshore programme. Some have been disarmed. The hulls are now painted grey rather than olive green as previously.

*Daphne class ("Najaden")* (Royal Danish Navy)

| | |
|---|---|
| **AB 25** | P 1225 |
| **AB 26** | P 1226 |
| **AB 27** | P 1227 |
| **AB 28** | P 1228 |
| **AB 29** | P 1229 |
| **AB 30** | P 1230 |
| **AB 31** | P 1231 |
| **AB 32** | P 1232 |
| **AB 33** | P 1233 |
| **AB 34** | P 1234 |
| **AB 35** | P 1235 |
| **AB 36** | P 1236 |

**Displacement, tons:** 170
**Dimensions, feet (metres):** 132 × 21 × 5.5 *(40.2 × 6.4 × 1.7)*
**Guns:** 2—40 mm (in some); 1—40 mm; 1—20 mm (others)
**A/S weapons:** 1 Mousetrap
**Main engines:** 4 MTU diesels; 2 shafts; 3 200 bhp
**Speed, knots:** 22
**Commissioned:** 1967-70

*AB 25 type ("AB 33") 9/1983 (*Selim Sam*)*

| | |
|---|---|
| **ANAGA** | PVZ 21 |
| **TAGOMAGO** | PVZ 22 |
| **MAROLA** | PVZ 23 |
| **MOURO** | PVZ 24 |
| **GROSA** | PVZ 25 |
| **MEDAS** | PVZ 26 |
| **IZARO** | PVZ 27 |
| **TABARCA** | PVZ 28 |
| **DEVA** | PVZ 29 |
| **BERGANTIN** | PVZ 210 |

**Displacement, tons:** 296.5 standard; 350 full load
**Dimensions, feet (metres):** 145.6 × 21.6 × 8.2 *(44.4 × 6.6 × 2.5)*
**Guns:** 1—76 mm Mk 22; 2—20 mm Mk 10; 2 MGs
**Main engine:** 1 MTU diesel; 4 300 hp = 22 knots (max), 20 (normal)
**Range, miles:** 4 000 at 13 knots
**Complement:** 25 (3 officers, 22 ratings)
**Commissioned:** 1980-82

Ordered from Bazán, Cádiz on 22 July 1978. For fishery and EEZ patrol duties.

Designed to release 'Lazaga' class for other operations.

Rescue and fire-fighting capability. Last pair laid down 15 December 1980. First pair launched January 1980, second pair 21 April 1980, next four 15 December 1980 and last pair 24 November 1981. Recently fitted with cp propellers.

*Anaga (old number) (1980* X. I. Taibo*)*

**BORA** (ex-USS *Surprise*)   P 339

**Displacement, tons:** 225 standard; 245 full load
**Dimensions, feet (metres):** 164.5 × 23.8 × 9.5
 *(50.1 × 7.3 × 2.9)*
**Guns:** 1—3 in *(76 mm)*/50 (Mk 34); 1—
 40 mm/60 (Mk 10); 4—.50 MGs
**Main engines:** CODAG; 2 Cummins diesels;
 1 450 hp = 16 knots; 1 GE gas turbine; 13 300
 shp = 40 knots
**Complement:** 25
**Commissioned:** 1969

This vessel belongs to the largest Patrol Type built
by the US Navy since the Second World War and
the first of that Navy to have gas turbines.
Transferred to Turkey on 28 February 1973.

*Asheville class ("Bora") 5/1983*
*(*Selim Sam*)*

| | |
|---|---|
| ATREVIDA | PA 61 |
| PRINCESA | PA 62 |
| NAUTILUS | PA 64 |
| VILLA DE BILBAO | PA 65 |

**Displacement, tons:** 1 031 standard; 1 135 full load
**Dimensions, feet (metres):** 247.8 × 33.5 × 9.8 *(75.5 × 10.2 × 3)*
**Guns:** 1—3 in *(76 mm)*/L50 (Mk 22); 3—40 mm/L70 (SP 48)
**Mines:** 20 can be carried
**Main engines:** Sulzer diesels; 2 shafts; 3 000 bhp = 18.5 knots
**Oil fuel, tons:** 105
**Range, miles:** 8 000 at 10 knots
**Complement:** 132 (9 officers, 123 men)
**Commissioned:** 1954-60

Survivors of a class of six.

All have been modernised, PA 61 in 1959-60, remainder while building. No funnel, the diesel exhaust being on the starboard side waterline. PA numbers allocated 1980 when they were rated as ocean-going patrol ships (patulleros de altura). A/S weapons removed.

**Aircraft:** Although no deck is fitted helicopters can be refuelled in flight.

**Radar:** Modified SPS 5B combined air/surface search.

**Refits:** All refitted 1979. Modernisation of engines and upper-works to maintain them in service for offshore patrol and fishery protection.

*Atrevida class ("Princesa") 7/1983*
*(G. Gyssels)*

| | |
|---|---|
| **BULGIA** | P 803 |
| **FREYR** | P 804 |
| **HADDA** | P 805 |

**Displacement, tons:** 169 standard; 225 full load
**Dimensions, feet (metres):** 119.1 × 20.2 × 6.3
  *(36.3 × 6.2 × 1.9)*
**Guns:** 2—20 mm (single)
**A/S weapons:** DCs (2 racks, 2 DCTs, 2 chutes)
**Main engines:** Diesels; 2 shafts; 1 300 shp = 15.5
  knots
**Range, miles:** 1 000 at 13 knots
**Complement:** 28
**Commissioned:** 1954-55

*Balder class ("Bulgia") 11/1985*
*(L & L van Ginderen)*

| | |
|---|---|
| CACINE | P 1140 |
| CUNENE | P 1141 |
| MANDOVI | P 1142 |
| ROVUMA | P 1143 |
| CUANZA | P 1144 |
| GEBA | P 1145 |
| ZAIRE | P 1146 |
| ZAMBEZE | P 1147 |
| LIMPOPO | P 1160 |
| SAVE | P 1161 |

**Displacement, tons:** 292.5 standard; 310 full load

**Dimensions, feet (metres):** 144 × 25.2 × 7.1 *(44 × 7.7 × 2.2)*

**Guns:** 1—40 mm; 1—32-barrelled 37 mm rocket launcher; 1—20mm

**Main engines:** 2 MTU 12V 538 Maybach (MTU) diesels; 4 000 bhp = 20 knots

**Range, miles:** 4 400 at 12 knots

**Complement:** 33 (3 officers, 30 men)

**Commissioned:** 1969-73

*Cacine class ("Mandovi") 1983*
*(L & L van Ginderen)*

**LEEDS CASTLE**                    P 258
**DUMBARTON CASTLE**               P 265

**Displacement, tons:** 1 427
**Dimensions, feet (metres):** 265.7 × 37.7 × 24;
  11.8 keel *(81 × 11.5 × 7.3; 3.6)*
**Gun:** 1—40 mm Mk 3 (fitted for but not with
  1—76 mm)
**Main engines:** 2 Ruston 12RKCM diesels; 2 cp
  propellers (230 rpm); 5 640 bhp = 19.5 knots
**Fuel, tonnes:** 180
**Range, miles:** 10 000 at 12 knots
**Complement:** 50 (plus austerity accommodation
  for 25 Royal Marines)
**Commissioned:** 1981-82

Ordered from Hall Russell and Co Ltd, Aberdeen
8 August 1980. Cost £10 million each. *Leeds
Castle* laid down November 1979 as a private
speculation, launched 29 October 1980,
completed 25 August 1981. *Dumbarton Castle*
launched 3 June 1981. Design includes an ability
to lay mines in war. Satellite terminal in *Leeds
Castle.*

**Aircraft:** Helicopter landing deck with refuelling
facilities for Sea King but no hanger.

*Castle class ("Leeds Castle") 1981*
*(Royal Navy)*

| | |
|---|---|
| SULTANHISAR | P 111 |
| DEMIRHISAR | P 112 |
| YARHISAR | P 113 |
| AKHISAR | P 114 |
| SIVRIHISAR | P 115 |
| KOÇHISAR | P 116 |

**Displacement, tons:** 280 standard; 412 full load
**Dimensions, feet (metres):** 173.7 × 23 × 10.2 *(53 × 7 × 3.1)*
**Guns:** 1—40 mm; 4—20 mm (twin)
**A/S weapons:** 4 DCTs; 1 Hedgehog (some in place of 40 mm gun)
**Main engines:** 2 FM diesels; 2 shafts; 2 800 bhp = 19 knots
**Range, miles:** 6 000 at 10 knots
**Complement:** 65 (5 officers, and 60 men)
**Commissioned:** 1964-65

Transferred in May 1964, 22 April 1965, September 1964, 3 December 1964, June 1965 and July 1965 respectively.

*PC 1638 class ("Kochisar") 4/1983*
*(Selim Sam)*

**AB 21** (ex-*PGM 104*)  P 1221
**AB 22** (ex-*PGM 105*)  P 1222
**AB 23** (ex-*PGM 106*)  P 1223
**AB 24** (ex-*PGM 108*)  P 1224

**Displacement, tons:** 130 standard; 147 full load
**Dimensions, feet (metres):** 101 × 21 × 7 *(30.8 × 6.4 × 2.1)*
**Guns:** 1—40 mm; 4—20 mm
**Main engines:** 2 diesels; 2 shafts; 1 850 hp = 18.5 knots
**Range, miles:** 1 500 at 10 knots
**Complement:** 15
**Commissioned:** 1967-68

*PGM 71 class ("AB 23") 6/1982*
*(L & L van Ginderen)*

| | |
|---|---|
| PEACOCK | P 239 |
| PLOVER | P 240 |
| STARLING | P 241 |
| SWALLOW | P 242 |
| SWIFT | P 243 |

**Displacement, tons:** 690 approx
**Dimensions, feet (metres):** 204.1 × 32.8 × 8.9
  *(62.6 × 10 × 2.7)*
**Guns:** 1—76 mm OTO Melara Compact;
  4—7.62 mm
**Main engines:** 2 Crossley Pielstick 18 PA6V 280
  diesels; reverse reduction gear boxes; 2 fixed
  pitch propellers; 14 000 bhp = 25 knots
**Auxiliary drive:** Retractable Schottel drive; 181
  hp
**Range, miles:** 2 500 at economical speed
**Complement:** 31 (accommodation for 44—6
  officers, 38 ratings)
**Commissioned:** 1984-85

This class is replacing the elderly 'Ton' class in Hong Kong, the colony's government paying 75 per cent of the cost. All ordered 30 June 1981.
  *Peacock* launched 1 December 1982, *Plover* on 12 April 1983, *Starling* on 11 September 1983, *Swallow* on 31 March 1984 and *Swift* on 11 September 1984. Carry two Sea Riders and telescopic cranes, have loiter drive and replenishment at sea equipment.

*Peacock class ("Peacock") 11/1983*
*(L & L van Ginderen)*

| | |
|---|---|
| **BEAR** | WMEC 901 |
| **TAMPA** | WMEC 902 |
| **HARRIET LANE** | WMEC 903 |
| **NORTHLAND** | WMEC 904 |
| **SPENCER** | WMEC 905 |
| **SENECA** | WMEC 906 |
| **ESCANABA** | WMEC 907 |
| **TAHOMA** | WMEC 908 |
| **CAMPBELL** | WMEC 909 |
| **THETIS** | WMEC 910 |
| **FORWARD** | WMEC 911 |
| **LEGARE** | WMEC 912 |
| **MOHAWK** | WMEC 913 |

**Displacement, tons:** 1 780 full load
**Dimensions, feet (metres):** 270 × 38 × 13.5 *(82.3 × 11.6 × 4.1)*
**Aircraft:** 1 HH-52A or 1 HH-65A or 1 LAMPS 3 helicopter
**Missiles:** (see note)
**Guns:** 1—3 in *(76 mm)*/62 (Mk 75)
**A/S weapons:** (see note)
**Main engines:** 2 Alco diesels; 2 shafts; 7 000 shp = 19.5 knots
**Range, miles:** 9 500 at 13 knots
**Complement:** 95 plus 19 aircrew when LAMPS is embarked
**Commissioned:** 1983-89

This class will replace the 'Campbell' class and other medium and high endurance cutters.

**Armament:** Weight and space reserved for Harpoon; 1 Phalanx 20 mm CIWS; Nixie Torpedo decoy.

**A/S weapons:** These ships have no shipboard A/S weapons, but rely on helicopters to deliver torpedoes against submarines detected by the ships' towed sonar array.

*Famous Cutter class ("Bear")*
*(US Coast Guard)*

| | |
|---|---|
| **HAMILTON** | WHEC 715 |
| **DALLAS** | WHEC 716 |
| **MELLON** | WHEC 717 |
| **CHASE** | WHEC 718 |
| **BOUTWELL** | WHEC 719 |
| **SHERMAN** | WHEC 720 |
| **GALLATIN** | WHEC 721 |
| **MORGENTHAU** | WHEC 722 |
| **RUSH** | WHEC 723 |
| **MUNRO** | WHEC 724 |
| **JARVIS** | WHEC 725 |
| **MIDGETT** | WHEC 726 |

**Displacement, tons:** 3 050 full load
**Dimensions, feet (metres):** 378 × 42.8 × 20
  *(115.2 × 13.1 × 6.1)*
**Helicopters:** 1 HH-52A or HH-3 helicopter
**Guns:** 1—5 in *(127 mm)*/38 (Mk 30); 2—40 mm;
  2—20 mm/Mk 67 MGs
**A/S weapons:** 2 triple torpedo tubes (Mk 32)
**Main engines:** Diesel or gas turbine (CODOG): 2
  diesels (Fairbanks-Morse); 7 000 bhp; 2 gas
  turbines (Pratt & Whitney FT- 4A); 36 000 shp;
  2 shafts; (cp propellers)
**Speed, knots:** 29, 20 cruising
**Oil fuel:** 800 tons
**Range, miles:** 14 000 at 11 knots (diesels); 2 400
  at 29 knots (gas)
**Complement:** 164 (15 officers, 149 enlisted)
**Commissioned:** 1967-72

**Design:** These ships have clipper bows, twin
funnels enclosing a helicopter hangar, helicopter
platform aft. All are fitted with oceanographic
laboratories, elaborate communications
equipment, and meteorological data gathering
facilities.

**Fleet Rehabilitation and Modernisation
Programme (FRAM):** In October 1985 a FRAM
programme for all 12 ships in this class was
started.

*Hamilton/Hero classes ("Munro")*
*(US Coast Guard)*

# Indexes

**NATO ship types and classes according to countries**

# Pennant list of major NATO surface ships

## Type abbreviations

| | |
|---|---|
| AVT | Auxiliary aircraft landing training ship |
| BB | Battleship |
| CA | Gun cruiser |
| CG | Guided missile cruiser |
| CGH | Light aircraft carrier |
| CGN | Guided missile cruiser (nuclear powered) |
| CL | Light cruiser |
| CLT | Light cruiser, training |
| CV | Multi-purpose aircraft carrier |
| CVA | Attack aircraft carrier |
| CVH | Helicopter carrier |
| CVL | Light aircraft carrier |
| CVN | Multi-purpose aircraft carrier (nuclear powered) |
| CVS | ASW aircraft carrier |

| | |
|---|---|
| DD | Destroyer |
| DDG | Guided missile destroyer (including surface to air missiles) |
| DDGH | Guided missile destroyer (helicopter) |
| DDH | Destroyer (helicopter) |
| FF | Frigate |
| FFG | Guided missile frigate (including surface to air missiles) |
| FFGH | Guided missile frigate (including surface to air missiles) (helicopter) |
| FFH | Frigate (helicopter) |
| FFL | Light frigate |
| LHA | Amphibious assault ship (general purpose) |
| LPH | Amphibious assault ship (helicopter) |

# Pennant numbers of major surface ships in numerical order

| Number | Ship's name | Type | Country | Number | Ship's name | Type | Country |
|---|---|---|---|---|---|---|---|
| R 01 | Dedalo | CVL | Spain | FFG 8 | McInerney | FFGH | USA |
| FFG 1 | Brooke | FFGH | USA | CGN 9 | Long Beach | CGN | USA |
| LHA 1 | Tarawa | LHA | USA | DDG 9 | Towers | DDG | USA |
| DDG 2 | Charles F. Adams | DDG | USA | FFG 9 | Wadsworth | FFGH | USA |
| FFG 2 | Ramsey | FFGH | USA | LPH 9 | Guam | LPH | USA |
| LHA 2 | Saipan | LHA | USA | DDG 10 | Sampson | DDG | USA |
| LPH 2 | Iwo Jima | LPH | USA | F 10 | Aurora | FFGH | UK |
| DDG 3 | John King | DDG | USA | FFG 10 | Duncan | FFGH | USA |
| FFG 3 | Schofield | FFGH | USA | LPH 10 | Tripoli | LPH | USA |
| LHA 3 | Belleau Wood | LHA | USA | DDG 11 | Sellers | DDG | USA |
| LPH 3 | Okinawa | LPH | USA | FFG 11 | Clark | FFGH | USA |
| DDG 4 | Lawrence | DDG | USA | LPH 11 | New Orleans | LPH | USA |
| FFG 4 | Talbot | FFGH | USA | R 11 | Principe de Asturias | CVH | Spain |
| LHA 4 | Nassau | LHA | USA | CVS 12 | Hornet | CVS | USA |
| R 05 | Invincible | CGH | UK | DDG 12 | Robison | DDG | USA |
| DDG 5 | Claude V. Ricketts | DDG | USA | F 12 | Achilles | FFGH | UK |
| FFG 5 | Richard L. Page | FFGH | USA | FFG 12 | George Philip | FFGH | USA |
| LHA 5 | Pelileu | LHA | USA | LPH 12 | Inchon | LPH | USA |
| D 06 | Aspis | DDG | Greece | DDG 13 | Hoel | DDG | USA |
| R 06 | Illustrious | CGH | UK | FFG 13 | Samuel Eliot Morison | FFGH | USA |
| DDG 6 | Barney | DDG | USA | DDG 14 | Buchanan | DDG | USA |
| FFG 6 | Julius A. Furer | FFGH | USA | FFG 14 | John H. Sides | FFGH | USA |
| R 07 | Ark Royal | CGH | UK | DDG 15 | Berkeley | DDG | USA |
| DDG 7 | Henry B. Wilson | DDG | USA | F 15 | Euryalus | FFGH | UK |
| FFG 7 | Oliver Hazard Perry | FFGH | USA | FFG 15 | Estocin | FFGH | USA |
| LPH 7 | Guadalcanal | LPH | USA | AVT 16 | Lexington | AVT | USA |
| DDG 8 | Lynde McCormick | DDG | USA | CG 16 | Leahy | CG | USA |

| Number | Ship's name | Type | Country | Number | Ship's name | Type | Country |
|--------|-------------|------|---------|--------|-------------|------|---------|
| D 16 | Velos | DDG | Greece | CG 24 | Reeves | CG | USA |
| DDG 16 | Joseph Strauss | DDG | USA | D 24 | Alcala Galiano | DD | Spain |
| F 16 | Diomede | FFGH | UK | DDG 24 | Waddell | DDG | USA |
| FFG 16 | Clifton Sprague | FFGH | USA | FFG 24 | Jack Williams | FFGH | USA |
| CG 17 | Harry E. Yarnell | CG | USA | CGN 25 | Bainbridge | CGN | USA |
| DDG 17 | Conyngham | DDG | USA | D 25 | Jorge Juan | DD | Spain |
| CG 18 | Worden | CG | USA | FFG 25 | Copeland | FFG | USA |
| DDG 18 | Semmes | DDG | USA | CG 26 | Belknap | CG | USA |
| F 18 | Galatea | FFGH | UK | FFG 26 | Gallery | FFGH | USA |
| CG 19 | Dale | CG | USA | CG 27 | Josephus Daniels | CG | USA |
| D 19 | Glamorgan | DDGH | UK | FFG 27 | Mahlon S. Tisdale | FFGH | USA |
| DDG 19 | Tattnal | DDG | USA | CG 28 | Wainwright | CG | USA |
| FFG 19 | John A. Moore | FFGH | USA | F 28 | Cleopatra | FFG | UK |
| CG 20 | Richmond K. Turner | CG | USA | FFG 28 | Boone | FFGH | USA |
| CVS 20 | Bennington | CVS | USA | CG 29 | Jouett | CG | USA |
| D 20 | Fife | DDGH | UK | FFG 29 | Stephen W. Groves | FFGH | USA |
| DDG 20 | Goldsborough | DDG | USA | CG 30 | Horne | CG | USA |
| FFG 20 | Antrim | FFGH | USA | FFG 30 | Reid | FFGH | USA |
| CG 21 | Gridley | CG | USA | CG 31 | Sterett | CG | USA |
| DDG 21 | Cochrane | DDG | USA | CVA 31 | Bon Homme Richard | CVA | USA |
| FFG 21 | Flatley | FFGH | USA | D 31 | Ierax | FFG | Greece |
| CG 22 | England | CG | USA | DDG 31 | Decatur | DDG | USA |
| D 22 | Almirante Ferrandiz | DD | Spain | F 31 | Descubierta | FFG | Spain |
| DDG 22 | Benjamin Stoddert | DDG | USA | FFG 31 | Stark | FFGH | USA |
| FFG 22 | Fahrion | FFGH | USA | CG 32 | William H. Standley | CG | USA |
| CG 23 | Halsey | CG | USA | DDG 32 | John Paul Jones | DDG | USA |
| D 23 | Almirante Valdes | DD | Spain | F 32 | Diana | FFG | Spain |
| D 23 | Bristol | DDG | UK | FFG 32 | John L. Hall | FFGH | USA |
| DDG 23 | Richard E. Byrd | DDG | USA | CG 33 | Fox | CG | USA |
| FFG 23 | Lewis B. Puller | FFGH | USA | F 33 | Infanta Elena | FFG | Spain |

| Number | Ship's name | Type | Country | Number | Ship's name | Type | Country |
|--------|-------------|------|---------|--------|-------------|------|---------|
| FFG 33 | Jarrett | FFGH | USA | D 42 | Kimon | DDG | Greece |
| CG 34 | Biddle | CG | USA | DDG 42 | Mahan | DDG | USA |
| CV 34 | Oriskany | CV | USA | F 42 | Phoebe | FFGH | UK |
| DDG 34 | Somers | DDG | USA | FFG 42 | Klakring | FFGH | USA |
| F 34 | Infanta Cristina | FFG | Spain | CV 43 | Coral Sea | CV | USA |
| FFG 34 | Aubrey Fitch | FFGH | USA | D 43 | Marques de la Ensenada | DDH | Spain |
| CGN 35 | Truxtun | CGN | USA | DDG 43 | Dahlgren | DDG | USA |
| F 35 | Cazadora | FFG | Spain | FFG 43 | Thach | FFGH | USA |
| CGN 36 | California | CGN | USA | DDG 44 | William V. Pratt | DDG | USA |
| F 36 | Vencedora | FFG | Spain | DDG 45 | Dewey | DDG | USA |
| FFG 36 | Underwood | FFGH | USA | F 45 | Minerva | FFGH | UK |
| CGN 37 | South Carolina | CGN | USA | FFG 45 | De Wert | FFGH | USA |
| DDG 37 | Farragut | DDG | USA | DDG 46 | Preble | DDG | USA |
| FFG 37 | Crommelin | FFGH | USA | FFG 46 | Rentz | FFGH | USA |
| CGN 38 | Virginia | CGN | USA | CG 47 | Ticonderoga | CG | USA |
| DDG 38 | Luce | DDG | USA | F 47 | Danae | FFGH | UK |
| F 38 | Arethusa | FFGH | UK | FFG 47 | Nicholas | FFGH | USA |
| FFG 38 | Curts | FFGH | USA | CG 48 | Yorktown | CG | USA |
| CGN 39 | Texas | CGN | USA | FFG 48 | Vandegrift | FFGH | USA |
| DDG 39 | MacDonough | DDG | USA | CG 49 | Vincennes | CG | USA |
| F 39 | Naiad | FFGH | UK | FFG 49 | Robert G. Bradley | FFGH | USA |
| FFG 39 | Doyle | FFGH | USA | CG 50 | Valley Forge | CG | USA |
| CGN 40 | Mississippi | CGN | USA | FFG 50 | Taylor | FFGH | USA |
| DDG 40 | Coontz | DDG | USA | CG 51 | Thomas S. Gates | CG | USA |
| F 40 | Sirius | FFGH | UK | DDG 51 | Arleigh Burke | DDG | USA |
| FFG 40 | Halyburton | FFGH | USA | FFG 51 | Gary | FFGH | USA |
| CGN 41 | Arkansas | CGN | USA | CG 52 | Bunker Hill | CG | USA |
| CV 41 | Midway | CV | USA | F 52 | Juno | FFGH | UK |
| DDG 41 | King | DDG | USA | FFG 52 | Carr | FFGH | USA |
| FFG 41 | McClusky | FFGH | USA | CG 53 | Mobile Bay | CG | USA |

| Number | Ship's name | Type | Country | Number | Ship's name | Type | Country |
|--------|-------------|------|---------|--------|-------------|------|---------|
| FFG 53 | Hawes | FFGH | USA | D 63 | Mendez Nuñez | DDH | Spain |
| CG 54 | Antietam | CG | USA | BB 64 | Wisconsin | BB | USA |
| D 54 | Leon | FFG | Greece | CV 64 | Constellation | CV | USA |
| FFG 54 | Ford | FFGH | USA | D 64 | Langara | DDH | Spain |
| CG 55 | Leyte Gulf | CG | USA | PA 64 | Nautilus | FF | Spain |
| FFG 55 | Elrod | FFGH | USA | CVN 65 | Enterprise | CVN | USA |
| CG 56 | Bennington | CG | USA | D 65 | Nearchos | DDG | Greece |
| D 56 | Lonchi | DDG | Greece | D 65 | Blas de Lezo | DDH | Spain |
| F 56 | Argonaut | FFGH | UK | PA 65 | Villa de Bilbao | FF | Spain |
| FFG 56 | Simpson | FFGH | USA | CV 66 | America | CV | USA |
| F 57 | Andromeda | FFGH | UK | CV 67 | John F. Kennedy | CV | USA |
| FFG 57 | Reuben James | FFGH | USA | D 67 | Panthir | FFG | Greece |
| F 58 | Hermione | FFGH | UK | CVN 68 | Nimitz | CVN | USA |
| FFG 58 | Samuel B. Roberts | FFGH | USA | CVN 69 | Dwight D. Eisenhower | CVN | USA |
| CV 59 | Forrestal | CV | USA | CVN 70 | Carl Vinson | CVN | USA |
| FFG 59 | Kauffman | FFGH | USA | F 70 | Apollo | FFGH | UK |
| CV 60 | Saratoga | CV | USA | CVN 71 | Theodore Roosevelt | CVN | USA |
| F 60 | Jupiter | FFGH | UK | F 71 | Baleares | FFG | Spain |
| FFG 60 | Rodney M. Davis | FFGH | USA | F 71 | Scylla | FFGH | UK |
| BB 61 | Iowa | BB | USA | CVN 72 | Abraham Lincoln | CVN | USA |
| CV 61 | Ranger | CV | USA | F 72 | Andalucia | FFG | Spain |
| D 61 | Churruca | DDH | Spain | F 72 | Ariadne | FFGH | UK |
| FFG 61 | Ingraham | FFGH | USA | CVN 73 | George Washington | CVN | USA |
| PA 61 | Atrevida | FF | Spain | F 73 | Cataluña | FFG | Spain |
| BB 62 | New Jersey | BB | USA | F 74 | Asturias | FFG | Spain |
| CV 62 | Independence | CV | USA | F 75 | Extremadura | FFG | Spain |
| D 62 | Gravina | DDH | Spain | F 75 | Charybdis | FFGH | UK |
| PA 62 | Princesa | FF | Spain | F 81 | Santa Maria | FFGH | Spain |
| BB 63 | Missouri | BB | USA | F 82 | Victoria | FFGH | Spain |
| CV 63 | Kitty Hawk | CV | USA | F 83 | Numancia | FFGH | Spain |

| Number | Ship's name | Type | Country | Number | Ship's name | Type | Country |
|--------|-------------|------|---------|--------|-------------|------|---------|
| D 85 | Sfendoni | DDG | Greece | D 108 | Cardiff | DDGH | UK |
| F 85 | Cumberland | FFGH | UK | F 109 | Leander | FFGH | UK |
| D 86 | Birmingham | DDGH | UK | F 126 | Plymouth | FFGH | UK |
| F 86 | Campbeltown | FFGH | UK | F 127 | Penelope | FFGH | UK |
| D 87 | Newcastle | DDGH | UK | CA 139 | Salem | CA | USA |
| F 87 | Chatham | FFGH | UK | F 169 | Amazon | FFGH | UK |
| D 88 | Glasgow | DDGH | UK | F 171 | Active | FFGH | UK |
| F 88 | Broadsword | FFGH | UK | F 172 | Ambuscade | FFGH | UK |
| D 89 | Exeter | DDGH | UK | F 173 | Arrow | FFGH | UK |
| F 89 | Battleaxe | FFGH | UK | F 174 | Alacrity | FFGH | UK |
| D 90 | Southampton | DDGH | UK | D 181 | Hamburg | DDG | Germany, Federal |
| F 90 | Brilliant | FFGH | UK | | | | |
| D 91 | Nottingham | DDGH | UK | D 182 | Schleswig-Holstein | DDG | Germany, Federal |
| F 91 | Brazen | FFGH | UK | | | | |
| D 92 | Liverpool | DDGH | UK | D 183 | Bayern | DDG | Germany, Federal |
| F 92 | Boxer | FFGH | UK | | | | |
| F 93 | Beaver | FFGH | UK | D 184 | Hessen | DDG | Germany, Federal |
| F 94 | Brave | FFGH | UK | | | | |
| D 95 | Manchester | DDGH | UK | D 185 | Lütjens | DDG | Germany, Federal |
| F 95 | London | FFGH | UK | | | | |
| D 96 | Gloucester | DDGH | UK | F 185 | Avenger | FFGH | UK |
| F 96 | Sheffield | FFGH | UK | D 186 | Mölders | DDG | Germany, Federal |
| D 97 | Edinburgh | DDGH | UK | | | | |
| R 97 | Jeanne d'Arc | CVH | France | D 187 | Rommel | DDG | Germany, Federal |
| D 98 | York | DDGH | UK | | | | |
| F 98 | Coventry | FFGH | UK | 206 | Saguenay | DDH | Canada |
| R 98 | Clemenceau | CVS | France | 207 | Skeena | DDH | Canada |
| F 99 | Cornwall | FFGH | UK | F 207 | Bremen | FFGH | Germany, Federal |
| R 99 | Foch | CVS | France | | | | |
| F 107 | Rothesay | FFGH | UK | F 208 | Niedersachsen | FFGH | Germany, Federal |

| Number | Ship's name | Type | Country | Number | Ship's name | Type | Country |
|--------|-------------|------|---------|--------|-------------|------|---------|
| F 209 | Rheinland-Pfalz | FFGH | Germany, Federal | 258 | Kootenay | DD | Canada |
| D 210 | Themistocles | DDGH | Greece | 259 | Terra Nova | DD | Canada |
| F 210 | Emden | FFGH | Germany, Federal | 261 | Mackenzie | DD | Canada |
| D 211 | Miaoulis | DDH | Greece | 262 | Saskatchewan | DD | Canada |
| F 211 | Köln | FFGH | Germany, Federal | 263 | Yukon | DD | Canada |
| | | | | 264 | Qu'Appelle | DD | Canada |
| D 212 | Kanaris | DDG | Greece | 265 | Annapolis | DDH | Canada |
| F 212 | Karlsruhe | FFGH | Germany, Federal | 266 | Nipigon | DDH | Canada |
| D 213 | Kountouriotis | DDG | Greece | 280 | Iroquois | DDGH | Canada |
| D 214 | Sachtouris | DDG | Greece | 281 | Huron | DDGH | Canada |
| D 215 | Tompazis | DDG | Greece | 282 | Athabaskan | DDGH | Canada |
| D 216 | Apostolis | DDG | Greece | 283 | Algonquin | DDGH | Canada |
| D 217 | Kriezis | DDG | Greece | F 300 | Oslo | FFG | Norway |
| F 222 | Augsburg | FF | Germany, Federal | F 301 | Bergen | FFG | Norway |
| | | | | F 302 | Trondheim | FFG | Norway |
| F 224 | Lübeck | FF | Germany, Federal | F 303 | Stavanger | FFG | Norway |
| | | | | F 304 | Narvik | FFG | Norway |
| F 225 | Braunschweig | FF | Germany, Federal | F 310 | Sleipner | FF | Norway |
| | | | | F 311 | Aeger | FF | Norway |
| 229 | Ottawa | DDH | Canada | D 340 | Istanbul | DD | Turkey |
| 230 | Margaree | DDH | Canada | F 340 | Beskytteren | FFH | Denmark |
| F 230 | Norfolk | FFGH | UK | D 341 | Izmir | DD | Turkey |
| 233 | Fraser | DDH | Canada | D 345 | Yucetepe | DD | Turkey |
| 234 | Assiniboine | DDH | Canada | D 346 | Alcitepe | DD | Turkey |
| 236 | Gatineau | DD | Canada | D 347 | Anittepe | DD | Turkey |
| F 240 | Yavuz | FFG | Turkey | D 348 | Savastepe | DD | Turkey |
| 257 | Restigouche | DD | Canada | F 348 | Hvidbjørnen | FFH | Denmark |
| | | | | D 349 | Kiliç Ali Paşa | DD | Turkey |
| | | | | F 349 | Vaedderen | FFH | Denmark |
| | | | | D 350 | Piyale Paşa | DD | Turkey |

| Number | Ship's name | Type | Country | Number | Ship's name | Type | Country |
|--------|-------------|------|---------|--------|-------------|------|---------|
| F 350 | Ingolf | FFH | Denmark | F 482 | Comandante Roberto Ivens | FF | Portugal |
| D 351 | M. Fevzi Çakmak | DD | Turkey | F 483 | Comandante Sacadura Cabral | FF | Portugal |
| F 351 | Fylla | FFH | Denmark | F 484 | Augusto de Castilho | FF | Portugal |
| D 352 | Gayret | DD | Turkey | F 485 | Honorio Barreto | FF | Portugal |
| F 352 | Peder Skram | FFG | Denmark | F 486 | Baptista de Andrade | FF | Portugal |
| D 353 | Adatepe | DD | Turkey | F 487 | João Roby | FF | Portugal |
| F 353 | Herluf Trolle | FFG | Denmark | F 488 | Afonso Cerqueira | FF | Portugal |
| D 354 | Kocatepe | DD | Turkey | F 489 | Oliveira E. Carmo | FF | Portugal |
| F 354 | Niels Juel | FFG | Denmark | C 550 | Vittorio Veneto | CGH | Italy |
| F 355 | Olfert Fischer | FFG | Denmark | D 550 | Ardito | DDGH | Italy |
| D 356 | Zafer | DD | Turkey | C 551 | Giuseppe Garibaldi | CVL | Italy |
| F 356 | Peter Tordenskiold | FFG | Denmark | D 551 | Audace | DDGH | Italy |
| DM 357 | Muavenet | DD | Turkey | C 553 | Andrea Doria | CLGH | Italy |
| D 358 | Berk | FF | Turkey | C 554 | Caio Duilio | CLGH | Italy |
| D 359 | Peyk | FF | Turkey | F 564 | Lupo | FFGH | Italy |
| D 360 | Gelibolu | DD | Turkey | F 565 | Sagittario | FFGH | Italy |
| D 361 | Gemlik | DD | Turkey | F 566 | Perseo | FFGH | Italy |
| F 450 | Elli | FFGH | Greece | F 567 | Orsa | FFGH | Italy |
| F 451 | Limnos | FFGH | Greece | D 570 | Impavido | DDG | Italy |
| F 471 | Antonio Enes | FF | Portugal | F 570 | Maestrale | FFGH | Italy |
| F 472 | Alm Pereira Da Silva | FF | Portugal | D 571 | Intrepido | DDG | Italy |
| F 473 | Alm Gago Coutinho | FF | Portugal | F 571 | Grecale | FFGH | Italy |
| F 474 | Alm Magalhaes Correa | FF | Portugal | F 572 | Libeccio | FFGH | Italy |
| F 475 | João Coutinho | FF | Portugal | F 573 | Scirocco | FFGH | Italy |
| F 476 | Jacinto Candido | FF | Portugal | F 574 | Aliseo | FFGH | Italy |
| F 477 | General Pereira d'Eca | FF | Portugal | F 575 | Euro | FFGH | Italy |
| F 480 | Comandante João Belo | FF | Portugal | F 576 | Espero | FFGH | Italy |
| | | | | F 577 | Zeffiro | FFGH | Italy |
| F 481 | Comandante Hermenegildo Capelo | FF | Portugal | F 580 | Alpino | FFH | Italy |
| | | | | F 581 | Carabiniere | FFH | Italy |

| Number | Ship's name | Type | Country | Number | Ship's name | Type | Country |
|--------|-------------|------|---------|--------|-------------|------|---------|
| F 594 | Virginio Fasan | FFH | Italy | F 748 | Protet | FFG | France |
| F 595 | Carlo Margottini | FFH | Italy | F 749 | Enseigne de Vaisseau Henry | FFG | France |
| D 602 | Suffren | DDG | France | F 781 | D'Estienne d'Orves | FFG | France |
| D 603 | Duquesne | DDG | France | F 782 | Amyot d'Inville | FF | France |
| D 609 | Aconit | DDG | France | F 783 | Drogou | FFG | France |
| D 610 | Tourville | DDGH | France | F 784 | Detroyat | FF | France |
| C 611 | Colbert | CLG | France | F 785 | Jean Moulin | FF | France |
| D 611 | Duguay-Trouin | DDGH | France | F 786 | Quartier Maitre Anquetil | FFG | France |
| D 612 | De Grasse | DDGH | France | F 787 | Commandant De Pimodan | FFG | France |
| D 614 | Cassard | DDGH | France | F 788 | Second Maitre Le Bihan | FF | France |
| D 615 | Jean Bart | DDGH | France | F 789 | Lieutenant de Vaisseau le Henaff | FF | France |
| D 616 | Courbet | DDGH | France | F 790 | Lieutenant de Vaisseau Lavallée | FF | France |
| D 625 | Dupetit Thouars | DDG | France | F 791 | Commandant L'Herminier | FF | France |
| D 627 | Maillé Brezé | DD | France | F 792 | Premier Maitre L'Her | FFG | France |
| D 628 | Vauquelin | DD | France | F 793 | Commandant Blaison | FFG | France |
| D 630 | Du Chayla | DDG | France | F 794 | Enseigne de Vaisseau Jacoubet | FFG | France |
| D 633 | Duperré | DDGH | France | F 795 | Commandant Ducuing | FFG | France |
| D 638 | La Galissonnière | DDH | France | F 796 | Commandant Birot | FFG | France |
| D 640 | Georges Leygues | DDGH | France | F 797 | Commandant Bouan | FFG | France |
| D 641 | Dupleix | DDGH | France | F 801 | Tromp | DDGH | Netherlands |
| D 642 | Montcalm | DDGH | France | F 806 | De Ruyter | DDGH | Netherlands |
| D 643 | Jean de Vienne | DDGH | France | F 807 | Kortenaer | FFGH | Netherlands |
| D 644 | Primauguet | DDGH | France | F 808 | Callenburgh | FFGH | Netherlands |
| D 645 | Lamotte Picquet | DDGH | France | F 809 | Van Kinsbergen | FFGH | Netherlands |
| F 725 | Victor Schoelcher | FFG | France | F 810 | Banckert | FFGH | Netherlands |
| F 726 | Commandant Bory | FFG | France | F 811 | Piet Heyn | FFGH | Netherlands |
| F 727 | Amiral Charner | FFG | France | F 812 | Jacob van Heemskerck | FFG | Netherlands |
| F 728 | Doudart de Lagrée | FFG | France | F 813 | Witte de With | FFG | Netherlands |
| F 729 | Balny | FF | France | F 814 | Isaac Sweers | FFGH | Netherlands |
| F 740 | Commandant Bourdais | FFG | France | F 815 | Evertsen | FFGH | Netherlands |

| Number | Ship's name | Type | Country | Number | Ship's name | Type | Country |
|--------|-------------|------|---------|--------|-------------|------|---------|
| F 816 | Abraham Crijnssen | FFGH | Netherlands | DD 973 | John Young | DDGH | USA |
| F 823 | Philips van Almonde | FFGH | Netherlands | DD 974 | Comte de Grasse | DDGH | USA |
| F 824 | Bloys van Treslong | FFGH | Netherlands | DD 975 | O'Brien | DDGH | USA |
| F 825 | Jan van Brakel | FFGH | Netherlands | DD 976 | Merrill | DDGH | USA |
| F 826 | Pieter Florisz | FFGH | Netherlands | DD 977 | Briscoe | DDGH | USA |
| F 910 | Wielingen | FFG | Belgium | DD 978 | Stump | DDGH | USA |
| F 911 | Westdiep | FFG | Belgium | DD 979 | Conolly | DDGH | USA |
| F 912 | Wandelaar | FFG | Belgium | DD 980 | Moosbrugger | DDGH | USA |
| F 913 | Westhinder | FFG | Belgium | DD 981 | John Hancock | DDGH | USA |
| DD 931 | Forrest Sherman | DD | USA | DD 982 | Nicholson | DDGH | USA |
| DD 937 | Davis | DD | USA | DD 983 | John Rodgers | DDGH | USA |
| DD 940 | Manley | DD | USA | DD 984 | Leftwich | DDGH | USA |
| DD 941 | Dupont | DD | USA | DD 985 | Cushing | DDGH | USA |
| DD 942 | Bigelow | DD | USA | DD 986 | Harry W. Hill | DDGH | USA |
| DD 943 | Blandy | DD | USA | DD 987 | O'Bannon | DDGH | USA |
| DD 944 | Mullinnix | DD | USA | DD 988 | Thorn | DDGH | USA |
| DD 946 | Edson | DD | USA | DD 989 | Deyo | DDGH | USA |
| DD 948 | Morton | DD | USA | DD 990 | Ingersoll | DDGH | USA |
| DD 950 | Richard S. Edwards | DD | USA | DD 991 | Fife | DDGH | USA |
| DD 951 | Turner Joy | DD | USA | DD 992 | Fletcher | DDGH | USA |
| DD 963 | Spruance | DDGH | USA | DDG 993 | Kidd | DDG | USA |
| DD 964 | Paul F. Foster | DDGH | USA | DDG 994 | Callaghan | DDG | USA |
| DD 965 | Kinkaid | DDGH | USA | DDG 995 | Scott | DDG | USA |
| DD 966 | Hewitt | DDGH | USA | DDG 996 | Chandler | DDG | USA |
| DD 967 | Elliott | DDGH | USA | DD 997 | Hayler | DDGH | USA |
| DD 968 | Arthur W. Radford | DDGH | USA | FF 1037 | Bronstein | FF | USA |
| DD 969 | Peterson | DDGH | USA | FF 1038 | McCloy | FF | USA |
| DD 970 | Caron | DDGH | USA | FF 1040 | Garcia | FFH | USA |
| DD 971 | David R. Ray | DDGH | USA | FF 1041 | Bradley | FFH | USA |
| DD 972 | Oldendorf | DDGH | USA | FF 1043 | Edward McDonnell | FFH | USA |

| Number | Ship's name | Type | Country | Number | Ship's name | Type | Country |
|--------|-------------|------|---------|--------|-------------|------|---------|
| FF 1044 | Brumby | FFH | USA | FF 1072 | Blakely | FFGH | USA |
| FF 1045 | Davidson | FFH | USA | FF 1073 | Robert E. Peary | FFGH | USA |
| FF 1047 | Voge | FFH | USA | FF 1074 | Harold E. Holt | FFGH | USA |
| FF 1048 | Sample | FF | USA | FF 1075 | Trippe | FFGH | USA |
| FF 1049 | Koelsch | FFH | USA | FF 1076 | Fanning | FFGH | USA |
| FF 1050 | Albert David | FF | USA | FF 1077 | Ouellet | FFGH | USA |
| FF 1051 | O'Callahan | FFH | USA | FF 1078 | Joseph Hewes | FFGH | USA |
| FF 1052 | Knox | FFGH | USA | FF 1079 | Bowen | FFGH | USA |
| FF 1053 | Roark | FFGH | USA | FF 1080 | Paul | FFGH | USA |
| FF 1054 | Gray | FFGH | USA | FF 1081 | Aylwin | FFGH | USA |
| FF 1055 | Hepburn | FFGH | USA | FF 1082 | Elmer Montgomery | FFGH | USA |
| FF 1056 | Connole | FFGH | USA | FF 1083 | Cook | FFGH | USA |
| FF 1057 | Rathburne | FFGH | USA | FF 1084 | McCandless | FFGH | USA |
| FF 1058 | Meyerkord | FFGH | USA | FF 1085 | Donald B. Beary | FFGH | USA |
| FF 1059 | W. S. Sims | FFGH | USA | FF 1086 | Brewton | FFGH | USA |
| FF 1060 | Lang | FFGH | USA | FF 1087 | Kirk | FFGH | USA |
| FF 1061 | Patterson | FFGH | USA | FF 1088 | Barbey | FFGH | USA |
| FF 1062 | Whipple | FFGH | USA | FF 1089 | Jesse L. Brown | FFGH | USA |
| FF 1063 | Reasoner | FFGH | USA | FF 1090 | Ainsworth | FFGH | USA |
| FF 1064 | Lockwood | FFGH | USA | FF 1091 | Miller | FFGH | USA |
| FF 1065 | Stein | FFGH | USA | FF 1092 | Thomas C. Hart | FFGH | USA |
| FF 1066 | Marvin Shields | FFGH | USA | FF 1093 | Capodanno | FFGH | USA |
| FF 1067 | Francis Hammond | FFGH | USA | FF 1094 | Pharris | FFGH | USA |
| FF 1068 | Vreeland | FFGH | USA | FF 1095 | Truett | FFGH | USA |
| FF 1069 | Bagley | FFGH | USA | FF 1096 | Valdez | FFGH | USA |
| FF 1070 | Downes | FFGH | USA | FF 1097 | Moinester | FFGH | USA |
| FF 1071 | Badger | FFGH | USA | FF 1098 | Glover | FF | USA |

# Named NATO ships

## Country abbreviations

| | | | | | | |
|---|---|---|---|---|---|
| Bel | Belgium | Gre | Greece | Spn | Spain |
| Can | Canada | Ita | Italy | Tur | Turkey |
| Den | Denmark | Ndl | Netherlands | UK | United Kingdom |
| Fra | France | Nor | Norway | USA | United States of America |
| GFR | Germany, Federal Republic | Por | Portugal | | |

# Classes

WINSTON Churchill    Black Hull  3 masted

Royalist    Black & white hull.  2  "

Malcolm Miller    Black hull  3 masted